Fried Rice

Fried Rice

50 Ways to Stir Up the World's Favorite Grain

Danielle Centoni

SASQUATCH BOOKS
SEATTLE

Contents

9   *Introduction*

11   *Tips, Tricks, and Techniques*

BUILDING BLOCKS AND GARNISHES

37   Steamed White Rice

38   Steamed Brown Rice

39   Kombu Dashi Rice

40   Lapsang Souchong Rice

42   Lemon Rice

42   Buttermilk Rice

43   Coconut Rice

44   Tomato Rice

47   Puffed Rice

48   Crispy Soy-Glazed Bonito Flakes (Okaka)

49   Japanese Soy-Preserved Kombu (Kombu Tsukudani)

49   Duck Leg Confit

51   Preserved Lemons

52   Middle Eastern Spice Mix

52   Shatta Sauce

ASIAN INSPIRATION

57   Classic Chinese Fried Rice with BBQ Pork

58   Spicy Fried Rice with Chinese Broccoli, Ground Pork, and
      Szechuan Chili Oil

60   Japanese Chahan with Shrimp, Dashi Rice, and Kombu Tsukudani

62   Smoky Lapsang Souchong Fried Rice with Duck Breast and Hoisin Sauce

64   Vietnamese Pho Fried Rice with Beef, Cilantro, and Bean Sprouts

67   Vietnamese Pork Meatball Banh Mi Fried Rice

69   Pad Thai Fried Rice with Shrimp and Spinach

72   Nam Khao Tod with Pork Larb

75   Thai Fried Coconut Rice with Pork Satay and Spinach

78   Burmese Fried Rice with Chicken, Herbs, and Crispy Shallots

80   Nasi Goreng (Indonesian Fried Rice)

82   Korean Kimchi and Bulgogi Fried Rice

84   Filipino Fried Rice (Sinangag) with Adobo Chicken

FLAVORS OF INDIA, AFRICA, AND THE MIDDLE EAST

89   Vagharelo Bhaat (Gujarati Fried Rice) with Chicken and Cilantro Yogurt

91   Chitranna (Indian Lemon Rice) with Curry Leaves and Cashews

93   Jollof Fried Rice with Chakalaka

95   Mujadara Fried Rice

99   Fried Cauliflower Rice with Turkey Kofta, Mint, and Feta

100   Moroccan Fried Rice with Chicken, Saffron, and Figs

103   Fried Rice with Halloumi, Pickled Onions, and Zhug

106   Lubia Polow (Persian Green Bean Rice with Beef)

CRUISING THROUGH EUROPE AND THE MEDITERRANEAN

112   Leek and Wild Mushroom Fried Rice

115   Salmon and Asparagus Fried Rice with Lemon and Fresh Dill

116   Hungarian Goulash Fried Rice with Paprika, Caraway, and Cabbage

118   Polish Fried Rice with Kielbasa and Cabbage

120   Duck Confit Fried Rice with Fennel, Mustard Greens, and Pickled Currants

123   Delicata and Kale Fried Rice with Rosemary, Agrodolce Raisins, and Parmesan

125   Carbonara Fried Rice

126   Shrimp "Scampi" Fried Rice with Spinach

128   Pancetta and Porcini Fried Risotto Balls (Arancini) with Fontina

131   Tuna Puttanesca Fried Rice

133   Paella Croquettes with Aioli

137   Grilled Greek Spanakorizo with Souvlaki Chicken

CLASSICS OF THE AMERICAS

143   Huevos Rancheros Fried Rice

145   Chorizo and Egg Fried Rice with Radishes and Avocado

146   New Mexican Chili Fried Rice with Queso and Pork

149   Buttermilk Buffalo Chicken Fried Rice

151   Cajun BBQ Shrimp Fried Rice

152   BBQ Fried Rice with Soy Curls and Spicy Slaw

155   Cheeseburger Fried Rice

157   Taco Salad Fried Rice

158   Ham and Cheese Fried Rice with Basil Pesto

161   Hawaiian Spam and Pineapple Fried Rice

163   Garlicky Bacon, Egg, and Avocado Fried Rice

165   Rainbow Veggie Fried Rice with Tofu

168   Bacon, Corn, and Crab Fried Rice with Sweet Peppers

A SWEET FINISH

172   Puffed-Rice PB & J Bars

174   Brown-Butter Apple and Cinnamon Fried Rice with Candied Nuts

175   New Orleans Calas with Spiced Sugar

177   Horchata Crepes with Bananas and Rum

180   Deep-Fried Rice Pudding

183   *Acknowledgments*

184   *Index*

Introduction

I've been to plenty of French restaurants that don't have *pain perdu* on the menu, same goes for Italian joints without *pappa al pomodoro* and Mexican restaurants without *chilaquiles*. They're classic dishes built on leftovers, ingenious in their use of stale bread and tortillas, but they're not necessarily a given.

And yet, I've never been to a Chinese restaurant that didn't serve fried rice. Built on cold leftover rice, it's a dish found everywhere, from cavernous dim sum palaces to tiny take-out joints—at least here in the States. Maybe that's because classic fried rice, with its cubes of sweet ham, squiggles of scrambled egg, and polka dots of green peas, is like the cozy sweatpants of Chinese cooking: familiar, flexible, and above all, deeply comforting.

No one really knows who invented Chinese fried rice, though legend has it that Emperor Yang of the Sui Dynasty kicked off the trend in the city of Yangzhou about 1,400 years ago. So it's had a long time to become entrenched in the world's culinary DNA, spreading throughout Asia and beyond. It seems wherever rice is grown or consumed, fried rice will follow.

Fast, cheap, and easy to make, it's no wonder the dish is so universally embraced. And wherever it goes, cooks give it their own spin, using ingredients they have on hand, whether it's fish sauce in Thailand or hot chilies in Indonesia. After all, that's the whole point of fried rice—to effortlessly turn your fridge leftovers and pantry staples into an entirely new dinner.

This book takes the virtues of fried rice—fast, cheap, customizable—and runs with it, using it as a blank slate for a whole world of flavors. Sure, there's a classic Chinese fried rice in these pages, but there's also Thai Fried Coconut Rice with Pork Satay and Spinach, Hungarian Goulash Fried Rice, and even Cheeseburger Fried Rice (trust me, it works). It turns out, almost anything that has a carb as its base, like pasta or sandwiches, can be turned into fried rice (heads up, gluten-free eaters), and if you already know a dish would taste good with rice, well, game on.

Most of the dishes in this book use plain white rice as the backdrop, but feel free to use other varieties that intrigue you, like brown or even black. And don't be afraid to change things up depending on what you have on hand; try mixing and matching components, swap out veggies as the seasons come and go, and let your own imagination come out and play.

As this book proves, there's really no limit to what you can do with fried rice. I've pulled inspiration from cuisines and traditions all over the world, so no matter what you're craving, you can give it the fried rice treatment and get it on the table fast.

Tips, Tricks, and Techniques

TYPES OF RICE

Browse your supermarket shelves, and you'll see at least half a dozen varieties of rice to choose from—from jasmine to basmati to jet-black Forbidden rice. Some packages don't even bother naming the variety and just cut to the chase with labels like "short-grain brown" or "long-grain white." But if you think that many choices is confusing, consider this: the UK-based Rice Association says there are more than forty thousand varieties of cultivated rice in the world.

Thankfully, we don't have to sift through that many options, but it's still not always obvious which rice to choose. Here's a primer to some of the most common rice varieties you'll encounter.

Long grain
Compared to short- or medium-grain rice, these are longer and more slender, not as sticky, and typically remain distinctly separate after cooking.

Rice starch is made up of amylose and amylopectin. It's the ratio of these two polysaccharides that determines a rice variety's stickiness. Long-grain rice has a higher proportion of amylose, which is the less sticky one. That's why the grains cook up fluffy and loose instead of clumpy.

Some labels you might see are Carolina and Texmati, but basmati and jasmine are the most well known. **Basmati** is an aromatic variety of long-grain rice with an almost nutty fragrance. It's strikingly more slender than regular long-grain rice, and it's most often used in Indian cooking.

Jasmine is also aromatic, but in a different way, almost like the grassy-coconut notes of *pandan* leaves. It's commonly used in Thai dishes and cooks up quite a bit stickier than basmati since it has a bit more amylopectin.

Because long-grain varieties of rice are so good at staying separate, they're ideal for using in fried rice, especially basmati.

Medium grain

Medium-grain rice varieties are just that: medium in length. The varieties that fit into this category usually have a little more amylopectin than long-grain varieties, so they tend to stick together a bit after cooking. Examples include **Calrose**, which was developed in California, and Japanese **sushi rice**.

Bhutanese red rice and black Chinese **Forbidden rice** are medium-grain varieties that are also incredibly healthful. They're a whole grain, like brown rice, since the bran and germ are intact, and they're rich in antioxidants thanks to the anthocyanins that give them their color. Forbidden rice cooks up into a beautiful dark-purple hue, which is cool on its own, but as a fried rice, it can look a bit murky. The solution? Top it with a big ol' fried egg, and marvel at how the whites of the egg really pop.

In a nutshell: Medium-grain rice may be a little stickier than long grain, but it still works perfectly for fried rice.

Short grain

Short-grain rices are stubby and almost round, and they usually have a much higher concentration of amylopectin, the sticky component of rice starch (although they still don't have as much as glutinous rice varieties). They also tend to absorb a lot more liquid.

Some varieties of short-grain rice include **arborio**, **carnaroli**, and **vialone nano**. These Italian varieties are known for having a high starch content, which helps create creamy risotto. Of the three,

arborio is the most well known, but carnaroli and *vialone nano* are considered the best because they're even starchier.

Bomba is a Spanish variety that looks similar, but it has less amylopectin than the traditional risotto rice varieties, so it doesn't get as sticky. That's why bomba is great for paella, for which you want distinct grains of rice.

Short-grain rice is great for the arancini and croquette recipes in this book. And if you want to make a "hippie" rice bowl with sticky clumps of brown rice, short grain is your friend. But if you're cooking up rice specifically for fried rice, it's best to stick with long or medium grain instead.

Parboiled/Converted

When you see this label, it just means that the rice was partially cooked first while it was still in its husk. Apparently, this infuses the grain with some of the flavor and nutrients from the bran and husk. It also gelatinizes the starches, so the rice grains remain separate and distinct after cooking. Then the grains are dried and polished like regular white rice. Uncle Ben's, probably the most famous brand of converted rice, uses a long-grain variety.

Glutinous

Contrary to its name, glutinous rice doesn't actually have gluten. It gets its name from its very sticky texture, caused by its high concentration of amylopectin. That stickiness is why this variety of rice is called "sticky rice" on menus. It's a staple of Southeast Asia, where it's used to sop up sauces like bread. But turning it into fried rice is a challenge since it's so sticky. One option is to let it dry out a bit and deep-fry it into crispy little clusters, using the puffed rice method on page 47.

Brown

Brown rice can be medium, long, or short. It just means the rice still has its germ and bran layer, though the husk has been removed. The bran and germ are responsible for brown rice's color, chewy texture, increased nutrients, and why it needs a longer cooking time.

Wild Rice

Technically, wild rice isn't rice; it's a grass, though It's cooked and used in much the same way. It's high in protein and nutrients and has a chewy texture and nutty taste. It doesn't have the same kind of starch as white rice, so it definitely performs differently. If you want to experiment with wild rice in your fried rice, by all means do, but it's best to use it as an accent. Wild rice is just too nutty and chewy to use on its own for fried rice.

BUYING AND STORING

The giant bags of rice at Costco or the Asian market are great deals, but they only make sense if you plan to eat rice on a frequent basis. Storing twenty pounds of rice for the long term requires plenty of space and airtight storage containers.

If you do want to stock up, transfer the rice to containers or bags that keep out air, moisture, and light. Think vacuum-sealed bags or jars, Mylar bags, or ziplock bags. Then store them in a cool, dark place.

For really long-term storage, tuck in a food-grade oxygen absorber (save them from packages you open or order them on online) to be sure it stays dry. And keep in mind that mice, rats, and even pantry pests can chew through plastic. So you might want to store the bags of rice in big plastic buckets with tight-fitting lids.

Now, don't be (too) alarmed, but oftentimes dry goods like rice can contain microscopic unhatched pest eggs. Usually, we cook with these things fast enough that the eggs never hatch (and let's be honest, we never even know they're there). But if you store the grains for a long time, eventually any eggs will hatch. To keep this from happening, freeze the rice (or flour or what have you) for a minimum of three days to kill the eggs once and for all.

Sometimes you'll see the words "new crop" and the year on bags of imported rice, particularly jasmine. This clue tells you the freshness of the rice, and the fresher the rice, the tastier it is and longer it'll keep.

Brown rice in particular needs to be protected from oxygen. The bran and germ contain natural oils that can go rancid within six months. If you need to store brown rice longer, tuck it in the fridge or freezer.

DAY-OLD IS BEST

Fried rice was invented to revitalize leftover cooked rice and use it up, but it's so delicious it would be sad to save it just for those occasions. Still, if you're going to cook up a fresh pot of rice just to fry it, you really should plan ahead. It's true what they say, day-old cold rice works best. It won't stick to the pan (at least not as much) and get broken or mushy.

If you don't have the time or patience to wait a day, at least try to wait about an hour. Just spread the cooked rice on a baking sheet until it's completely cool.

COOKING LIQUID

Water is, of course, traditional for cooking rice, but you can use just about anything. For savoriness, add broth or tea. For bright citrus flavor, use lemon juice. Try adding a sachet of whole herbs or aromatics. And even creamy liquids work, especially coconut milk. The natural fat will result in grains that glisten and remain separate, as if they've been spritzed with oil. Keep in mind that when you cook with something other than water, any particles in the liquid will adhere to the outside of the rice (such as tomato pulp or proteins in meat-based broths and dairy milks). Although flavorful, this results in stickier rice that's harder to fry. That's why I use vegetable broth instead of meat broth, and only sub out a cup of water for dairy.

How Much Liquid to Use?

Rule number 1: Forget what the rice package says. For some reason, most packages of rice recommend a lot more liquid than necessary, resulting in wet, mushy rice that's not ideal for frying.

Rule number 2: If you double the amount of rice, *don't* automatically double the amount of water. For example, if you cooked 1 cup of rice in 1¾ cups of water, don't assume you need 3½ cups water to cook 2 cups of rice. You actually only need 2¾ cups water.

Here's why: All rice requires a 1:1 ratio of rice to liquid in order to cook through. Rice *can* absorb more liquid, particularly some varieties of short-grain rice, but the point is that rice doesn't have to have more than an equal amount of liquid to become tender. Any extra liquid is added to account for the inevitable evaporation during the cooking process. Generally, ¾ cup extra liquid will work perfectly, though depending on your cooking method you might need a little more or a little less.

The amount of liquid that will evaporate mostly depends on how long the rice will need to cook. Brown rice takes about twice as long as white rice, so it needs a little more liquid. It can be hard to judge how much extra liquid to use when cooking brown rice, but generally, you just need about ¼ cup to ½ cup more water than you'd use for white rice to account for the evaporation during its longer cooking time. The foolproof way to cook it is to treat it like pasta: boil it in plenty of water, then drain it.

Evaporation also depends on your pot, how tight the lid fits, how long you let the water boil, et cetera. Still, as a rule of thumb, use a 1:1 ratio of rice to liquid, then add ¾ cup more liquid for white rice, and 1 to 1¼ cups more liquid for brown.

If you'd rather not do any math, try this tried-and-true trick employed by home cooks all over Asia: add just enough water so that it covers the rice by 1 inch. As a guide, place the tip of your finger on top of the rice. The water should reach to your first joint, which is about 1 inch from your fingertip. Just don't use a really wide pot, which will throw things off.

YIELD

Different varieties of rice will swell to different sizes when cooked, but generally, 2 cups of uncooked long- or medium-grain rice will yield 4 to 6 cups when cooked. When making fried rice, count on using 1 cup of cooked rice per person.

TO RINSE OR NOT TO RINSE?

Definitely rinse. Unless you're making risotto, where you want to retain the starch, it's always a good idea to rinse off as much of the

surface starch as possible so that the rice won't cook up too sticky and mushy. Rinsing in three changes of water is good enough. Don't go knocking yourself out, because the water will never be fully clear.

SALT YOUR RICE, BUT NOT TOO MUCH

When cooking rice to use in a fried rice dish, don't go overboard on the salt, since you'll likely be adding salty ingredients like soy sauce and fish sauce later on. If you start with already-salty rice, you'll have a very salty dish. Generally, ½ teaspoon of salt per cup of rice will do.

LET IT STEAM

For the fluffiest grains, you need to give the rice time to steam off some of the liquid it absorbed. Once all the liquid is absorbed and the rice is tender, remove the pot from the heat, take off the lid, and cover the pot with a dish towel. The dish towel keeps the heat inside while absorbing some of the steam and letting the rest pass through. Allow to sit for 10 minutes before gently fluffing with a fork, taking care not to break or mash the grains.

COOKING METHODS

RICE COOKERS: These tabletop appliances take the guesswork out of cooking rice and range in price from about $20 to more than $200, depending on the assortment of features. The main advantage of rice cookers is that you can click a button and walk away.

STOVE: Cooking rice on the stovetop is just about as easy as using a rice cooker, and you won't have to find room in your cupboards for yet another appliance. Just set the pot on medium-high heat and wait until it comes to a boil. Soon as it does, reduce the heat to low and cover with a lid. Waiting to cover the pot means you don't run the risk of boil-overs.

White rice will be cooked in 15 minutes, about 30 for brown. Remove from heat, remove the lid from the pot, cover with a dish towel, and allow to steam for 10 minutes before fluffing with a fork.

MICROWAVE: This is a great option when you don't have space on the stove, and it shaves a few minutes off the process too. Use a large, 2-quart glass measuring cup with a silicone lid, or a glass baking dish with a lid (be sure to lift a corner to allow steam to escape). Also, Asian markets sell special microwave rice cookers fairly cheap. With the microwave method, I use a little less water for evaporation than usual, about ½ cup instead of ¾ cup, since it doesn't cook as long. Just be sure your cooking vessel isn't more than half full. Boil-overs are the biggest issue with microwaving. To keep them to a minimum, cover and microwave at full power (I use a standard 1,100-watt microwave) for 7 minutes, or until the water is boiling and frothy. Then reduce to 30 percent power and microwave for 7 minutes more, until the water is absorbed and the rice is tender. Keep in mind that there's a lot of trial and error with this. The more rice and water, the longer it'll take, and every cooking vessel performs differently. After cooking, cover with a dish towel and let the rice steam for 10 minutes before fluffing with a fork.

INSTANT POT / ELECTRIC PRESSURE COOKERS: These appliances save a few minutes, but there's no evaporation, so stick with the 1:1 ratio of rice to water, with no added liquid. You can use the "Rice" button for white rice. For brown rice, use the manual mode and cook it for about 20 minutes. Let the pressure release naturally for 10 minutes,

then manually release the remaining pressure. Remove the lid, cover with a dish towel, and allow the rice to steam for 10 minutes before fluffing with a fork.

OVEN: When you're cooking rice for a big crowd, the oven is your friend. With the oven method, a little more steam escapes, so I add 1 cup of water for evaporation instead of ¾ cup. Preheat the oven to 375 degrees F, heat the liquid on the stove, and place the rice in a large roasting pan. When the liquid comes to a boil, pour it into the rice, cover tightly with foil, and bake for about 20 minutes until the liquid is absorbed. Remove from heat, remove the cover, drape a clean dish towel on top, and allow to steam for 10 minutes before fluffing with a fork.

FREEZING RICE

You can freeze cooked rice in quart- or gallon-size freezer bags so it's ready whenever you are. Make sure it's cold first, and wet your measuring cup so the rice doesn't stick to it. Once the bag is full, squeeze out the air, flatten, and seal. Arrange the bags on a baking sheet so they'll freeze flat, label with the contents and date, and freeze. Frozen rice will keep for several months in the freezer.

It's best to allow the rice to at least partially defrost in the fridge before frying so that it's easier to break up the grains.

A Note about Stir-Frying

Fried rice is basically stir-fried rice, which means it's traditionally cooked in a wok. But most of us don't have the right kind of burner to do wok cooking justice, and we might not have room to store a wok either.

Luckily, stir-frying in a sauté pan works great too; it just requires a slightly different technique to keep things from burning or overcooking. You see, in a wok you can push some ingredients up the sides of the pan away from heat while you stir-fry other ingredients at the bottom. This won't work in the big flat bottom of a sauté pan. That's why many of the recipes in this book instruct you to cook the ingredients in shifts and transfer them to a bowl or plate as they finish cooking. When everything is cooked, you can add those ingredients back into the pan.

To keep dishes to a minimum, I use the same sauté pan to cook everything, and often don't wipe it out in between steps. The exception is when scrambling eggs for fried rice. Sometimes you can clear some space in the pan and scramble them right there, but more often than not, it's easier to just bust out a little nonstick sauté pan and cook them separately.

COOKING TOOLS

LARGE (14-INCH) SAUTÉ PAN: To cook enough fried rice for four people, opt for the biggest pan you have, about 14 inches works great. Nonstick pans and well-seasoned cast-iron pans are best because they keep sticking to a minimum without requiring a ton of oil.

A traditional sauté pan is just fine, but it will require lots of additional oil to keep the rice from sticking, which could make the end result greasy. When I use a traditional sauté pan, I go easy on the oil and just embrace the stickiness. Eventually, the stuck-on film of rice starch on the bottom will start to lift off and you can incorporate those crunchy bits into the dish. Anything left in the pan dissolves quickly with a 5-minute soak in hot water.

SMALL (8-INCH) NONSTICK PAN: For frying or scrambling eggs, toasting nuts and spices, and making crepes.

HEAVY-BOTTOMED 4- TO 6-QUART SAUCEPAN WITH LID: This is big enough to cook rice for four people and great for deep-frying too.

DUTCH OVEN (6-QUART): An enameled or very well seasoned cast-iron or nonstick Dutch oven is essential for making the Lubia Polow on page 106 and for baking the risotto on page 128. But it's also versatile enough to use for cooking rice or even deep-frying. A plain stainless steel Dutch oven is prone to sticking.

RIMMED BAKING SHEETS: Great for holding breaded arancini at the ready for frying, and when lined with paper towels, they're the perfect spot to allow the fried rice balls or puffed rice to drain after cooking.

FINE-MESH SIEVE: For rinsing and straining rice, straining cooking oil, et cetera.

FINE-MESH SKIMMER: Look for these at Asian markets, they have a finer screen than regular wire skimmers, which makes them perfect for lifting puffed rice out of hot oil.

SLOTTED SPOON: For removing ingredients from the pan and leaving the oil behind.

CHEF'S KNIFE: For prepping ingredients, obviously. Just be sure to keep it nice and sharp.

FOOD PROCESSOR: For pureeing sauces, pestos, and batters. In some cases a blender will work too.

HANDHELD MANDOLINE: Not essential but nice to have for creating paper-thin slices of ingredients like fennel.

MORTAR AND PESTLE: A low-tech, superefficient way to grind whole spices or ingredients into powders and pastes.

MICROPLANE ZESTER GRATER: Essential for finely grating ginger and zesting citrus.

INSTANT-READ THERMOMETER: This tool is essential for making sure oil is at the right temperature for deep-frying (not to mention ensuring meats are cooked to the proper temperature). I love the Thermapen brand, which is what many chefs use. It's far more expensive than dial thermometers, but it's precise, super fast, compact, durable, and worth every penny.

STOCK THE PANTRY

BONITO FLAKES: Also known as *katsuobushi*, bonito flakes are made from dried, sometimes fermented, smoked tuna that is shaved into paper-thin flakes. They have a deeply savory, smoky, and fishy flavor. They're often sold in a 5-pack of 1-ounce packets. A Japanese cooking staple, they're easy to find in the international foods aisle of the supermarket or at Asian markets.

BRAGG LIQUID AMINOS: A staple of natural food stores, Bragg Liquid Aminos is like soy sauce, but different. Made with just soy and water, it doesn't taste as salty as soy sauce and has a deeply savory, almost coffee-like note. I throw it in anything that needs a bass note of depth, like braised greens.

CALABRIAN CHILIES: Hot but not searingly so, with a bright, fruity flavor, these chilies come from the Calabria region of Italy. You can buy crushed Calabrian chilies in oil at gourmet markets or online retailers. Use them anywhere you would crushed red pepper flakes.

CHINKIANG VINEGAR (CHINESE BLACK VINEGAR): Look for this bold and savory vinegar at Asian markets. It's extremely versatile, able to add both acidity and deep savory flavor at the same time.

CHIPOTLES IN *ADOBO*: Chipotles are simply smoked and dried jalapeños. For this Mexican cooking staple, the chipotles are simmered in adobo, which in Mexican cuisine is a rich red chili sauce (Filipino adobo is very different). The result is spicy, smoky, and super flavorful. Look for cans or jars of chipotles in adobo in the Mexican foods aisle. If you open a can and don't use the entire thing, freeze the leftovers in ice cube trays, adding one chipotle and a little sauce per cube. When frozen, just pop the cubes in a ziplock bag.

CHORIZO (SPANISH AND MEXICAN): Spanish chorizo is made with chopped pork and pork fat, garlic, and a heavy hit of *pimentón*, or smoked paprika. The sausages are dry-cured or smoked until they're firm and shelf stable. They can be sliced or diced and sautéed or simply eaten like a salami. In the United States, Mexican-style chorizo is usually a very soft fresh sausage made with ground pork and sometimes beef, heavily seasoned with chili powders and other spices. It's sold refrigerated and cooks up into a crumble. Soyrizo mimics this Mexican-style chorizo, but is made with soy instead of meat and tends not to be as rich.

DIAMOND CRYSTAL KOSHER SALT: Believe it or not, the kind of salt you cook with can make a big difference, and I'm not just talking about fancy flavored finishing salts. The trouble is that different brands of salt come in different-size flakes. So the bigger the flakes, the less salt fits in your measuring spoon. That means if you use a fine-grain salt when the recipe was developed with a bigger-flake salt, you'll end up with far saltier results because more salt fit in your spoon. All the recipes in this book were developed with Diamond Crystal Kosher Salt, which is available at most, if not all, supermarkets in a telltale red-and-white box. The flakes are light yet coarse, great for pinching and tossing into whatever you're making. If you use a finer grain salt, start by using about half of what the recipe specifies and adjust according to your taste. You want to add enough salt to make the flavors pop, but not so much that the dish tastes actually salty.

FISH SAUCE: Don't limit this funky salty liquid to Asian dishes. A few squirts of fish sauce can deepen flavor and add umami to everything from pasta sauce to clam chowder. I prefer Red Boat brand.

FRIED ONIONS OR SHALLOTS: Fried onions or shallots are a great topper for fried rice, adding both crunch and oniony flavor at the same time. Of course you can fry your own, but buying them saves a lot of time. Look for tubs at Asian markets or look for the Lars Own Crispy Onions at well-stocked supermarkets.

GOCHUGARU (HOT): These Korean red pepper flakes come in several spice levels. The hot variety is similar to red pepper flakes but not nearly as seedy and coarse. They're great for spicing things up and essential for Szechuan chili oil if you can't find Szechuan pepper flakes.

GOCHUJANG: A Korean red pepper paste that adds a slightly sweet-hot funk to stir-fry sauces and marinades. It's become so mainstream, you can now find it at many supermarkets.

HALLOUMI: A mild, semisoft cheese traditionally made in Cyprus from a blend of goat and sheep milk. It's salty, a little tangy, and excellent for grilling because it browns beautifully and gets deliciously soft while still retaining its shape. Look for it at well-stocked supermarkets and Middle Eastern markets.

HOISIN SAUCE: A thick, dark sweet-sour sauce made with fermented soybeans, sugar, garlic, and spices. It's commonly used in marinades and stir-fry sauces, and is easy to find at most supermarkets and Asian markets.

INDIAN CHILI POWDER: Bright-red and made with Kashmiri chilies, Indian chili powder is similar in heat level to cayenne but more flavorful. Look for it at Indian and Middle Eastern markets.

KECAP MANIS: This sweet, syrupy-thick soy sauce is commonly used in Indonesian cooking. Good kecap manis is made with palm sugar and aromatics like ginger, garlic, and dried chilies. Look for it at Asian markets. Or you can make your own by simmering equal parts soy sauce and palm sugar or dark brown sugar (plus flavorings of your choice) until reduced, thick, and syrupy (about 10 minutes).

KIMCHI: Essential to Korean cuisine, kimchi is mainly cabbage (though other vegetables can be used) fermented with salt, flavorings, and Korean chili flakes (gochugaru). The funkiness and heat level vary by brand. Look for kimchi in the refrigerated section at the supermarket, often near the tofu.

KOMBU: These dried sheets of edible kelp are essential for making dashi. A Japanese cooking staple, kombu is easy to find in the international foods aisle of the supermarket or at Asian markets.

MIRIN· The real stuff is Japanese rice wine that is naturally sweeter and lower in alcohol than sake. But real mirin is hard to find, even in Asian markets. Most supermarkets carry "aji-mirin," a product that tastes essentially the same but is actually a blend of alcohol, water, and sugar or corn syrup. It's kind of like the difference between vanilla extract and artificial vanilla flavor. Either one will work in these recipes, so don't knock yourself out trying to find the real deal (unless you want to). Dry sherry will often work great too.

NAM PRIK PAO: This Thai roasted red chili paste is a sticky, sweet-spicy-funky blend of chilies, tamarind, fish sauce, shrimp paste, garlic, and shallots and is deeply flavorful. It adds incredible complexity to Thai dishes, like the Nam Khao Tod with Pork Larb on

with a tingly sensation. It's wild. And addictive. It also means your mouth can handle even more spice than usual. Look for them at spice shops or at Asian markets, where they might be labeled "prickly ash" after the tree they're harvested from. The brighter the peppercorns, the fresher they are; and it's really the husk you're after, not the brown seed inside. Toasting them before use brings out their flavor.

TAMARIND CONCENTRATE (LIQUID): For authentic pad Thai flavor, you need the sweet-sour fruity taste of tamarind concentrate. It's useful in marinades and even barbecue sauces too. Find it at Asian markets, the international foods aisle at some supermarkets, or spice shops like the Spice House.

THAI RED CURRY PASTE: Used as the base for Thai red curry sauce, the paste is a flavorful blend of red chilies, lemongrass, galangal, garlic, shallot, and makrut lime. It's easy to find in the international foods aisle of the supermarket.

TRUFFLE SALT: Look for real-deal truffle salt, made by blending ground dried truffles with sea salt. It's expensive, but a little goes a long way. Oregon-made Jacobsen Salt Co. and the Spice House are two good sources.

YUZU ESSENCE: This cold-pressed juice from the yuzu fruit is a very tart, fragrant, grapefruit-like fruit often used in Japanese cuisine. Yuzu essence tastes a bit like a cross between a tangerine, lemon, and grapefruit. The yuzu essence from Japan Gold USA can be found at well-stocked supermarkets or online retailers.

Building Blocks and Garnishes

Before you heat up your sauté pan or wok, you need to steam up some rice. Of course, white rice is the go-to blank canvas that works with everything, but you don't need to stop there. Several of the dishes in this book start with rice that's been custom-cooked to make that particular recipe pop. Think rich, tangy buttermilk rice that's perfect with spicy buffalo chicken, or lemony rice that's the ideal backdrop for a Greek-inspired dish. In this section, you'll also find a versatile spice mix, spicy sauce, and a few other components to help you cook up a next-level meal.

Steamed White Rice

You don't need a rice cooker to make perfect rice. You just need to use the right ratio and give it time to steam off the heat. And the ratio couldn't be easier—one part rice to one part liquid. Then, no matter if you're making one batch or a triple batch, just add ¾ cup more liquid to account for the evaporation during cooking. Keep in mind that other cooking methods use a little less or a little more water for evaporation. If you're not cooking rice on the stove, check the Cooking Methods on page 20.

MAKES ABOUT 6 CUPS

| 2 cups white rice (long or medium grain) | 2¾ cups water |
| 1 teaspoon kosher salt |

▪ Pour the rice into a medium, heavy-bottomed pot. Rinse with cold water, drain in a fine-mesh sieve, and repeat two more times to remove some of the surface starch.

→

- Return the rinsed rice to the pot, and add the water and salt. Bring just to a boil over medium-high heat, stir to ensure the rice isn't sticking to the bottom of the pot, cover, and reduce heat to low. Cook for 15 minutes.

- Remove from heat, remove the lid, and place a clean dish towel over the top. Allow the rice to steam for 10 to 15 minutes. Fluff with a fork and allow to cool before refrigerating.

Steamed Brown Rice

Since it has its bran and germ intact, brown rice is a whole grain, with more nutrients than regular white rice. But the bran and germ also give it a nuttier flavor and heartier texture that can be a bit overwhelming. To lighten things up but still pack in some nutrients, I mix equal parts brown and white rice to get the best of both worlds. They have to be cooked separately, though, since brown rice takes a little longer. It usually needs a little extra water too, since more water will evaporate during cooking. The trouble is, too much water and it'll end up mushy. To cut out the guesswork, it's best to cook brown rice like pasta. It works perfectly every time.

MAKES ABOUT 6 CUPS

2 cups brown rice (long or medium grain)	12 cups water
	1 teaspoon kosher salt

- Rinse the rice in a fine-mesh sieve (it won't have as much surface starch as white, so you don't need to triple-rinse it).

- Bring the water to a boil in a 4- to 6-quart pot over medium-high heat. Add the rice, stir, and cook for 25 to 30 minutes, uncovered, until al dente. Strain through the fine-mesh sieve set over the sink. Immediately return the rice to the pot, cover, and allow it to steam for 10 to 15 minutes, or until completely cooked through. Fluff with a fork and allow to cool before refrigerating.

Kombu Dashi Rice

Kombu dashi is a simple Japanese seaweed broth that's often used as the basis for soups, like miso, or the pancake-like *okonomiyaki*, where its flavor adds a beguiling savory, umami note. And it works great as the cooking water for rice too. The resulting rice tastes subtly oceanic, especially when fried with a handful of shrimp. The kombu and bonito flakes don't sit in the water long, so they still have plenty of flavor after they're pulled out. Instead of tossing them, spend a couple of extra minutes turning them into flavorful toppings for fried rice.

MAKES ABOUT 6 CUPS

6 cups cold water

1 (6-inch by 5-inch) piece dried kombu (Japanese dried kelp), rinsed

2 (5-gram) packets bonito flakes (dried fermented tuna flakes; ¼ cup)

2 cups white rice (long or medium grain)

1 tablespoon white miso paste

½ teaspoon kosher salt

▪ In a large saucepan, combine water and kombu. Cover and bring to a boil over medium-high heat. Once it boils, remove from heat and use tongs to remove the kombu; reserve to make *tsukudani* (Japanese Soy-Preserved Kombu; page 49).

▪ Add the bonito flakes and allow to steep for 5 minutes. Strain broth through a fine-mesh sieve over a large bowl, pressing on the bonito flakes to extract the excess liquid. Reserve the bonito flakes to make *okaka* (Crispy Soy-Glazed Bonito Flakes; page 48). The broth can be made several days ahead and refrigerated, or frozen for longer storage.

▪ Pour the rice into the saucepan, or use a medium, heavy-bottomed pot. Rinse with cold water, drain in a fine-mesh sieve, and repeat two more times to remove some of the surface starch.

▪ Return the rinsed rice to the pot and stir in 2¾ cups kombu broth, miso paste, and salt. Bring just to a boil over medium-high heat, stir to ensure the rice isn't sticking to the bottom of the pot, cover, and reduce heat to low. Cook for 15 minutes.

→

- Remove from heat, remove the lid, and place a clean dish towel over the top. Allow the rice to steam for 10 to 15 minutes. Fluff with a fork and allow to cool before refrigerating.

Lapsang Souchong Rice

Just a handful of this smoky black tea can transform your rice into something deeply aromatic and savory. Use it anywhere a smoky note would be welcome.

MAKES ABOUT 6 CUPS

3½ cups cold water	2 cups white rice (long or medium
¼ cup loose-leaf Lapsang souchong	grain)
tea	1 teaspoon kosher salt

- Bring the water to a boil in a medium, heavy-bottomed pot, covered, set over medium-high heat. Remove from heat and add the tea. Allow to steep for 5 minutes. Pour tea-water through a fine-mesh sieve into a large measuring cup. You should have about 3 cups. Discard the tea leaves, making sure no leaves are left in the pot.

- Pour the rice into the pot. Rinse with cold water, drain in a fine-mesh sieve, and repeat two more times to remove some of the surface starch.

- Return the rinsed rice to the pot and add 2¾ cups of the tea-steeped water and salt (you can discard or drink the remaining water). Bring just to a boil over medium-high heat, stir to ensure the rice isn't sticking to the bottom of the pot, cover, and reduce heat to low. Cook for 15 minutes.

- Remove from heat, remove the lid, and place a clean dish towel over the top. Allow the rice to steam for 10 to 15 minutes. Fluff with a fork and allow to cool before refrigerating.

Lemon Rice

A generous shot of fresh lemon juice gives rice a juicy brightness, and to round out the sharp citrus edges, I combine it with broth instead of water. Meat-based broths contain protein, which makes rice cook up stickier, so I use vegetable broth when making rice for frying.

MAKES ABOUT 6 CUPS

2 cups white rice (long or medium grain)
2½ cups low-sodium vegetable broth
Zest of 1 medium lemon

¼ cup freshly squeezed lemon juice (from about 1 medium lemon)
½ teaspoon kosher salt

▪ Pour the rice into a medium, heavy-bottomed pot. Rinse with cold water, drain in a fine-mesh sieve, and repeat two more times to remove some of the surface starch.

▪ Return the rinsed rice to the pot, and add the broth, lemon zest, lemon juice, and salt. Bring just to a boil over medium-high heat, stir to ensure the rice isn't sticking to the bottom of the pot, cover, and reduce heat to low. Cook for 15 minutes.

▪ Remove from heat, remove the lid, and place a clean dish towel over the top. Allow the rice to steam for 10 to 15 minutes. Fluff with a fork and allow to cool before refrigerating.

Buttermilk Rice

Similar to cooking rice in coconut milk, buttermilk adds richness to rice, with a subtle hit of tanginess as well. This is especially good with the spicy buffalo and ranch flavors of the Buttermilk Buffalo Chicken Fried Rice recipe on page 149.

MAKES ABOUT 6 CUPS

2 cups white rice (long or medium grain)
1½ cups water

1¼ cups buttermilk
1 teaspoon kosher salt

- Pour the rice into a medium, heavy-bottomed pot. Rinse with cold water, drain in a fine-mesh sieve, and repeat two more times to remove some of the surface starch.

- Return the rinsed rice to the pot, and add the water, buttermilk, and salt. Bring just to a boil over medium-high heat, stir to ensure the rice isn't sticking to the bottom of the pot, cover, and reduce heat to low. Cook for 15 minutes.

- Remove from heat, remove the lid, and gently stir to evenly incorporate the buttermilk solids. Place a clean dish towel over the top. Allow the rice to steam for 10 to 15 minutes. Fluff with a fork and allow to cool before refrigerating.

Coconut Rice

Cooking rice in rich, fatty coconut milk results in grains that are almost luxurious in flavor and texture. Some recipes use just a little coconut milk, but I go all in and use the whole can for maximum coconut flavor (plus, I don't want any leftovers). Use coconut rice in any dish with Southeast Asian flavors. It's great in desserts too.

MAKES ABOUT 6 CUPS

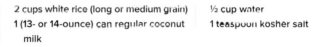

| 2 cups white rice (long or medium grain) | ½ cup water |
| 1 (13- or 14-ounce) can regular coconut milk | 1 teaspoon kosher salt |

- Pour the rice into a medium, heavy-bottomed pot. Rinse with cold water, drain in a fine-mesh sieve, and repeat two more times to remove some of the surface starch.

- Return the rinsed rice to the pot, and add the coconut milk, water, and salt. Bring just to a boil over medium-high heat, stir to ensure the rice isn't sticking to the bottom of the pot, cover, and reduce heat to low. Cook for 15 minutes.

- Remove from heat, remove the lid, and place a clean dish towel over the top. Allow the rice to steam for 10 to 15 minutes. Fluff with a fork and allow to cool before refrigerating.

Tomato Rice

Rice infused with tomato flavor is incredibly versatile. Use it as a base for the Cheeseburger Fried Rice on page 155, as well as the Jollof Fried Rice with Chakalaka on page 93. It would even be great in the Huevos Rancheros Fried Rice (page 143). Some of the tomato solids in the juice have a tendency to float to the top during cooking and coat the grains, but it's easy to stir them in.

MAKES ABOUT 6 CUPS

2 cups white rice (long or medium grain)
2 cups tomato juice

¼ cup water
1 teaspoon kosher salt

- Pour the rice into a medium, heavy-bottomed pot. Rinse with cold water, drain in a fine-mesh sieve, and repeat two more times to remove some of the surface starch.

- Return the rinsed rice to the pot, and add the tomato juice, water, and salt. Bring just to a boil over medium-high heat, stir to ensure the rice isn't sticking to the bottom of the pot, cover, and reduce heat to low. Cook for 15 minutes.

- Remove from heat, remove the lid, and gently stir to evenly incorporate the tomato solids. Place a clean dish towel over the top. Allow the rice to steam for 10 to 15 minutes. Fluff with a fork and allow to cool before refrigerating.

Puffed Rice

Word to the wise: this is crazy addictive. The rice has loads more flavor and better texture than both puffed rice and crisped rice cereals, and it's an awesome snack when sprinkled with Japanese *shichimi togarashi*. Of course it's also excellent in crisped rice treats, like the Puffed Rice PB & J Bars on page 172. I've experimented with several different methods and found that cooked rice that's been allowed to mostly, but not completely, dry out will retain the perfect amount of moisture to puff up, but not so much moisture that the puffs will be chewy. If your rice doesn't puff up at all, it's too dry.

MAKES ABOUT 6 CUPS

2 cups cold cooked white rice
4 cups vegetable oil

▪ Preheat oven to 200 degrees F. Spread the rice evenly on a baking sheet and place in the oven for about 1 hour. It should feel hard and crispy, but it should not have taken on any color. Remove and keep at room temperature in an airtight container until ready to try. (Rice can be prepared up to this point a week or two ahead.)

▪ Heat the vegetable oil in a deep, 6-quart, heavy-bottomed saucepan until it reaches 400 degrees F. Set a baking sheet lined with several layers of paper towels nearby. Add a handful of rice to the hot oil (break up any clumps with your hands first). Within a second or two, the rice will immediately puff and float to the top. Scoop it out with a fine-mesh skimmer and transfer to the prepared baking sheet. Repeat with the remaining rice. When cool, store the puffed rice in an airtight container. It'll keep for several days before it starts to taste stale.

NOTE: It's important that the oven temperature is no more than 200 degrees F; otherwise, the rice will start to brown. You can dry the rice at a lower temperature, but it will take longer. For old-fashioned ovens with a pilot light, you can let the rice dry out in the oven overnight. To determine when the rice is ready for frying, it's better to err on the side of a little too moist than too dry. You'll know your rice is too dry if it doesn't puff. Just try again with new rice and bake it for less time.

Crispy Soy-Glazed Bonito Flakes (*Okaka*)

You might think the soggy bonito flakes left over from making dashi aren't good for anything but the compost bin, but in Japan they're ingeniously turned into a quick savory garnish. Try sprinkling this umami-packed topping over fried rice, stir-fries, and soups.

MAKES ABOUT ⅓ CUP

Bonito flakes left over from making
dashi broth (page 39)

2 teaspoons mirin

2 teaspoons soy sauce

½ to 1 teaspoon Korean pepper
powder (*gochugaru*), or 1 pinch of
ground cayenne

1 tablespoon toasted sesame seeds

▪ Roughly chop the wet bonito flakes. Heat a small nonstick sauté pan over medium heat. Add the bonito flakes and cook, stirring, until dry and flaky, about 4 minutes. Add the mirin, soy sauce, and pepper powder to taste. Cook, stirring until mixture is evenly coated, the liquid has cooked off, and the flakes seem dry again, about 2 minutes. Remove from heat and stir in the sesame seeds. Allow to cool, then transfer to an airtight container. *Okaka* will keep for 2 weeks.

Japanese Soy-Preserved Kombu (Kombu *Tsukudani*)

When it comes to foods rich in umami, kombu ranks near the top. So it would be a shame to toss it out after making dashi. Just slice it up and let it braise in a soy-sauce-based mixture until it absorbs all the savory goodness. It's an addictive snack as is, or strew it atop anything that needs a hit of flavor.

MAKES ABOUT ½ CUP

1 (6-inch by 5-inch) piece soaked kombu from making kombu dashi, (or rinse dry kombu and soak in hot water for 10 minutes), cut crosswise into ⅓-inch-thick strips (about ½ cup)

1 cup cold water
3 tablespoons soy sauce
2 tablespoons rice vinegar
½ teaspoon granulated sugar

- Combine all ingredients in a small saucepan. Bring to a simmer over medium-high heat. Reduce heat to medium-low and gently cook, stirring occasionally, until liquid evaporates and kombu is very tender, about 30 minutes. Allow to cool, then refrigerate in an airtight container. It will keep for 2 weeks.

Duck Leg Confit

Although I do take the traditional step of dry brining the duck legs to remove moisture and concentrate the flavor, this is not the fully French, super-traditional way to confit a leg of duck. That's mainly because I use olive oil in addition to the rendered duck fat—since buying several cups of duck fat ain't cheap. But it works great and is a technique I use when making *carnitas* too, which is essentially pork confit (with different flavorings, of course). If you have any rendered duck fat from searing duck breasts for the recipe on page 62, feel free to use it here.

MAKES 4 SERVINGS

2 tablespoons kosher salt
2 teaspoons black peppercorns
3 large cloves garlic, smashed, divided
6 sprigs fresh thyme, divided

1 bay leaf
4 duck legs with thighs
Extra-virgin olive oil, as needed for cooking

→

- In a spice grinder or small food processor, pulse the salt, pepper, 1 clove of the garlic, 3 sprigs of thyme, and bay leaf until finely chopped. Sprinkle about a tablespoon of the mixture in the bottom of an 8-inch glass baking dish. Rub the remaining mixture all over the duck legs. Arrange the legs, skin side up, in the dish. Cover and refrigerate for 24 hours.

- Preheat oven to 275 degrees F. Brush the excess salt from the duck legs. Set large cast-iron skillet over medium-high heat. Add the duck legs and cook until fat starts to render. Turn the legs over, add the remaining 2 cloves of garlic and 3 sprigs of thyme, and enough olive oil (and any melted duck fat you might have on hand) until the legs are three-quarters of the way submerged. Cover the pan with aluminum foil and bake until the meat is nearly falling apart tender, about 2 hours.

- Allow to cool in the fat and refrigerate, covered, until ready to use. It will keep, submerged in fat, for several weeks.

- To use for fried rice, remove the legs from the fat, remove the skin, and pull the meat off the bone and shred or chop. Dice the skin, and sauté it in a hot pan until crispy. Fold the meat into the fried rice, and use the crispy skin as a garnish. To serve the legs whole, you can also reheat them in the oven at 400 degrees F until warm, then crisp the skin under the broiler or in a sauté pan. After using the duck meat, don't throw away the fat. It's very flavorful and great for sautéing or roasting vegetables—especially potatoes.

Preserved Lemons

Preserved lemons have a unique salty-bright-bitter flavor that's a wonderful counterpoint to savory dishes. You can keep these super simple—just lemons and salt—or add a few whole spices for even more complexity. Just be sure to use a sterilized jar (see note), and make sure the lemons are completely covered in salty juice. You can use the brine anywhere you want a hit of salty acid, so don't throw it out when you've used up all the lemons. To use the lemons, scrape off the mushy flesh and either discard or stir it into the dish, but the peel is the real prize. Just chop or slice as you see fit.

MAKES 1 PINT

5 to 6 small lemons or Meyer lemons	Optional spices: peppercorns, cloves,
Kosher salt	cinnamon stick, coriander seeds,
Freshly squeezed lemon juice	bay leaves

▪ Cut five of the lemons in quarters from top to bottom, but not all the way through. Spoon about a tablespoon of the salt into each lemon, rubbing it into the flesh, then squeeze the lemon back together.

▪ Sprinkle another tablespoon of salt into the bottom of the sterilized jar. Add the salted lemons, pushing and squishing them to fit tightly and sprinkling more salt and spices between them as you go. As you squish, they will release juices, which is a good thing. If the amount of juice released doesn't end up covering the lemons, add enough freshly squeezed lemon juice from the remaining lemon to cover.

▪ Screw on the lid and let the lemons ferment at room temperature, shaking the jar a couple of times a day in the beginning to encourage the salt to dissolve. Wait a month before using. Preserved lemons don't need to be refrigerated, but you can if it makes you nervous. They should keep for at least 6 months.

NOTE: To sterilize canning jars and lids, place in boiling water for 10 minutes.

Middle Eastern Spice Mix

This blend takes its cue from *advieh*, a Persian spice blend that varies from region to dish to cook. But no matter how many spices people use, advieh is always built on cinnamon, cardamom, and cumin. This version adds turmeric for a bit more earthiness and clove for complexity.

MAKES ABOUT ¼ CUP

2 tablespoons ground cumin

1 tablespoon plus 1 teaspoon ground cinnamon

2 teaspoons ground turmeric

2 teaspoons ground cardamom

1 teaspoon ground cloves

1 teaspoon freshly ground black pepper

- Combine ingredients in a small bowl or jar with an airtight lid. Keep in a cool, dry, dark place and try to use within 6 months.

Shatta Sauce

This thick hot sauce is similar to Israeli *zhug* or Moroccan harissa, but the additions of tomato paste, vinegar, and parsley set it apart. I also fry it in a little bit of oil to concentrate its flavors. It's essential for topping *koshari*, the national dish of Egypt (see Koshari Variation, page 96).

MAKES 2 CUPS

1 cup water

1 cup fresh Italian parsley (packed)

1 cup fresh cilantro (packed)

1 (6-ounce) can tomato paste

6 cloves garlic

1 large jalapeño pepper (or 2 small), stemmed

1 serrano pepper, stemmed

2 tablespoons red wine vinegar

1 teaspoon kosher salt

1 teaspoon freshly ground black pepper

1 teaspoon ground cumin

1 teaspoon ground coriander

2 tablespoons extra-virgin olive oil

- Puree all ingredients except olive oil in a blender or food processor until relatively smooth. Heat the olive oil in a medium saucepan set over medium heat. Add the puree (be careful; it will splatter), and cook, stirring occasionally, for about 10 minutes, until flavors meld and sauce has thickened slightly. Remove from the heat and allow to cool. (Sauce will keep refrigerated for several days.)

Asian Inspiration

/I\ \I/ /I\ \I/ /I\ \I/ /I\ \I/ /I\ \I/ /I\ \I/ /I\ \I/ /I\ \I/

Rice serves as the starchy backbone to all of Asia's cuisines, and where there's leftover rice, there's fried rice. Generally, the traditional recipes from this part of the world are all variations on the classic Chinese theme, whether they're from Japan, Thailand, or the Philippines. But cooks from each country are pulling from a slightly different pantry, and that's where things get interesting. Fried rice in Thailand will surely have fish sauce and chilies. In Japan, it's often made with short-grain rice and topped with nori. The recipes in this section dive even deeper into those culinary differences and spin a few other Asian classics into fried rice form.

/I\ \I/ /I\ \I/ /I\ \I/ /I\ \I/ /I\ \I/ /I\ \I/ /I\ \I/ /I\ \I/

Classic Chinese Fried Rice with BBQ Pork

No fried rice book would be complete without this Chinese take-out classic. *Char siu* is the perfect sweet-savory fit for the delicately seasoned rice, and it's easy to get at Asian markets and even the deli section at many mainstream grocery stores. But if you can't find it, ham or Chinese sausage work great, or just use whatever leftovers you have on hand. That's really the point of fried rice, after all.

MAKES 4 SERVINGS

2 teaspoons vegetable oil

1 medium yellow onion, diced

2 large cloves garlic, minced

8 ounces char siu (Chinese barbecued pork), diced

4 cups cold cooked rice

2 eggs, beaten

Kosher salt

1 tablespoon plus 2 teaspoons soy sauce

2 teaspoons sesame oil

2 teaspoons mirin

1½ cups frozen peas and carrots

- Heat 1 teaspoon of the oil in a large sauté pan over medium-high heat. Add the onion and sauté until tender, about 5 minutes. Add the garlic and sauté 1 minute more. Add the char siu and rice. Sauté until rice is warmed through and softened, then continue sautéing until the rice seems firm again, about 3 minutes.

- Push the rice to the side of the pan, and heat another teaspoon of oil in the cleared area. Add the beaten eggs, season with salt, and cook, stirring, until scrambled and cooked through. Stir into the rice. (If your pan doesn't seem big enough, scramble the eggs in a separate pan.)

- In a small bowl, combine the soy sauce, sesame oil, and mirin. Drizzle over the rice mixture, stirring until evenly combined. Add the frozen peas and carrots and cook until warmed through. Season with salt to taste.

- Divide rice among bowls and serve.

Spicy Fried Rice with Chinese Broccoli, Ground Pork, and Szechuan Chili Oil

My love for Szechuan wontons in chili oil is deep and everlasting. I could truly eat a bowlful every day. Maybe even several times a day. So I devised this rice as a shortcut to getting my fix. Once you have the chili oil made, it comes together fast. This recipe yields more chili oil than you'll need for one batch of fried rice, but it's so good you'll soon find dozens of uses for it. It's seriously simple to make, though it takes a little time on the stove and tastes even better after a day, so plan ahead.

MAKES 4 SERVINGS

SZECHUAN CHILI OIL

1 cup vegetable oil

1 (2-inch) piece fresh ginger, sliced into coins (no need to peel it)

4 cloves garlic, smashed

4 star anise

3 bay leaves

3 green cardamom pods, smashed

1 cinnamon stick

½ cup Szechuan chili flakes or coarse Korean red pepper flakes (*gochugaru*)

2 tablespoons Szechuan peppercorns

2 teaspoons kosher salt, or more to taste

2 teaspoons soy sauce

FRIED RICE

1 teaspoon Szechuan peppercorns, or more to taste

1 tablespoon vegetable oil, divided

5 green onions, ends trimmed, white and light-green parts chopped, dark-green parts finely chopped and reserved for garnish

3 large cloves garlic, minced

1 (2-inch) piece fresh ginger, peeled and grated (1 tablespoon)

1 pound ground pork

1 tablespoon Chinkiang vinegar (Chinese black vinegar)

1 teaspoon kosher salt

12 stalks *gai lan* (Chinese broccoli), cut diagonally into 1-inch lengths

1 medium yellow onion, chopped

4 cups cold cooked rice

1 tablespoon soy sauce

½ cup chopped unsalted roasted peanuts

■ **TO MAKE THE CHILI OIL:** In a small saucepan, combine the oil, ginger, garlic, star anise, bay leaves, cardamom pods, and cinnamon stick. Bring just to a bare simmer over medium heat, reduce to low, and very slowly simmer (at about 250 degrees F) until ginger and garlic are toasted and browned and oil is very fragrant, about 30 minutes.

■ Meanwhile, combine red pepper flakes, Szechuan peppercorns, and salt in a medium metal bowl. Set a fine-mesh sieve on top. When the oil is ready, increase heat to medium-high until the ingredients are sizzling. Remove from heat and immediately pour through the sieve into the bowl of pepper flakes. The flakes should sizzle and foam. Stir in the soy sauce. Discard the ingredients in the sieve. Allow the oil to cool, then taste and adjust with more salt if desired. Transfer to an airtight container and refrigerate (oil will keep in the refrigerator for months).

■ **TO MAKE THE FRIED RICE:** Heat a large sauté pan over medium-high heat. Add the Szechuan peppercorns and toast for about 30 seconds, until fragrant. Grind into a powder with a mortar and pestle or spice grinder. Set aside.

■ Heat 1 teaspoon of the oil in the sauté pan over medium-high heat, and add the green onions, garlic, and ginger. Sauté until fragrant, about 1 minute. Add the pork and sauté, stirring to break up the meat, until the pork is no longer pink, 3 to 5 minutes. Season with the vinegar and salt. Transfer to a plate.

■ Heat another teaspoon of oil in the pan, and add the *gai lan*. Sauté until the *gai lan* is tender-crisp, about 2 minutes. Transfer to the plate with the pork.

■ Heat the remaining teaspoon of oil in the pan over medium-high heat, and add the onion. Sauté until tender, about 5 minutes. Add the rice and sauté until warmed through and softened, then continue sautéing until the rice seems firm again, about 3 minutes. Add the pork and vegetables from the plate. Drizzle with the soy sauce and sauté, stirring until evenly distributed and ingredients are warmed through.

■ Divide rice among plates and top with chopped peanuts, a generous drizzle of chili oil, a pinch of ground Szechuan peppercorns, and remaining chopped green onions.

Japanese Chahan with Shrimp, Dashi Rice, and Kombu Tsukudani

Japanese fried rice (*chahan*) is almost identical to Chinese fried rice, complete with scrambled egg and soy sauce. The difference has more to do with the ingredients typically available on hand. In Japan, fried rice might come mixed with octopus and bonito flakes instead of pork and peas. This recipe uses ingredients typically found in Japanese cooking and doubles down on the briny, oceanic flavors of kombu, or dried Japanese kelp. It's used to flavor the cooking water for the rice and then braised into a salty-savory garnish.

MAKES 4 SERVINGS

2 tablespoons low-sodium tamari or soy sauce

2 tablespoons sake or dry sherry

1 tablespoon sesame oil

2 teaspoons white miso paste

2 teaspoons bottled yuzu essence

6 cloves garlic, minced or grated on a Microplane, divided

2 teaspoons grated ginger

1 pound peeled and deveined medium shrimp

1 tablespoon plus 1 teaspoon vegetable oil, divided

4 ounces shiitake mushrooms, stemmed, caps quartered (or chopped if large)

Kosher salt and freshly ground black pepper

1 medium yellow onion, diced

4 cups cold Kombu Dashi Rice (page 39)

1 cup frozen peas and carrots

2 green onions, ends trimmed, thinly sliced

½ cup Kombu Tsukudani, chopped (page 49)

⅓ cup Crispy Soy-Glazed Bonito Flakes (page 48)

▪ In a medium bowl, mix the tamari, sake, sesame oil, miso paste, yuzu essence, 2 teaspoons of the garlic, and ginger until fully combined. Add the shrimp and allow to marinate while you sauté the vegetables.

▪ Heat 1 teaspoon of the vegetable oil in a large sauté pan over medium-high heat. Add the mushrooms, season with salt and pepper, and allow to sear, stirring occasionally, until browned and juices have evaporated, about 3 minutes. Transfer to another medium bowl.

- Heat 1 teaspoon of oil in the same sauté pan over medium-high heat. Use a slotted spoon to remove half the shrimp from the marinade, letting the excess drip off. Add the shrimp to the pan and sauté until pink and cooked through and browned in places, 3 to 5 minutes. Transfer to the bowl with the mushrooms. Add another teaspoon of oil and repeat with the remaining shrimp; transfer to the bowl.

- Add the shrimp marinade to the same sauté pan and bring to a simmer over medium heat. Simmer for about 30 seconds. Transfer to a small bowl.

- Heat the remaining teaspoon of oil in the same sauté pan over medium-high heat. Add the onion and sauté until tender, about 5 minutes. Add the remaining garlic and sauté about 1 minute more. Add the rice and sauté until warmed through and softened, then continue sautéing until the rice seems firm again, about 3 minutes. Add the simmered marinade and stir until rice is evenly coated. Add the shrimp and mushrooms from the bowl and the peas and carrots. Sauté until warmed through. Taste and season with salt.

- Divide rice among bowls and garnish with green onions, *tsukudani*, and glazed bonito flakes.

Smoky Lapsang Souchong Fried Rice with Duck Breast and Hoisin Sauce

Sort of a shortcut riff on tea-smoked duck, this luxurious dish pairs rice cooked in smoky Lapsang souchong tea with seared duck breasts and a sweet-savory drizzle of hoisin sauce. Look for duck breasts in the freezer section at the supermarket. Better yet, buy a whole frozen duck (they're far cheaper) and cut the breasts and legs off yourself. Trust me, it's not hard. You can use the legs for the French-inspired Duck Confit Fried Rice on page 120, and simmer the carcass into duck broth. If that's too tall an order, feel free to use pork tenderloin or buy a roast Pekin duck from the Asian market and chop it up.

MAKES 4 SERVINGS

1 Pekin or Muscovy duck breast (about ½ pound)

8 ounces shiitake mushrooms, stemmed, caps quartered (or chopped if large)

Kosher salt and freshly ground black pepper

3 small baby bok choy, thinly sliced crosswise, with the stems kept separate

1 medium yellow onion, diced

4 large cloves garlic, minced

2 to 3 Thai chilies, minced

4 cups cold Lapsang Souchong Rice (page 40)

Vegetable oil, as needed for sautéing

2 eggs, beaten

1 cup frozen peas and carrots

1 tablespoon plus 1 teaspoon plum sauce

1 tablespoon soy sauce

1 tablespoon hoisin sauce

1 tablespoon Chinese black vinegar (chinkiang)

1 (2-inch) piece fresh ginger, peeled and grated (1 tablespoon)

¼ teaspoon Chinese five-spice powder

2 green onions, ends trimmed, thinly sliced

▪ If necessary, trim the duck breasts so that the skin isn't hanging over the meat (you can chop the excess skin and sauté it along with the breasts until crispy, then use as a garnish). Use a sharp knife to make shallow diagonal slashes in the skin, about ½ inch apart, making sure not to cut into the meat. Rotate the breasts and cut again to make a crisscross pattern (this will help the fat render).

▪ Set a large sauté pan over medium-low heat, and add the duck breast skin side down. Allow the duck to slowly cook for 8 to 10 minutes, until the fat has rendered and skin is brown and crispy. Turn over and cook the other side for another

8 to 10 minutes, until a thermometer inserted inside registers 155 degrees F. Remove from heat. Transfer the duck breast to a cutting board, and pour the rendered fat from the pan into a small bowl. When the meat is cool enough to handle, dice the breast into small bite-size pieces, skin and all. Set aside.

- Heat 1 teaspoon of the reserved duck fat in the same sauté pan. Add the mushrooms and season with salt and pepper. Allow to sear, stirring occasionally, until browned and juices have evaporated, about 3 minutes. Transfer to a medium bowl.

- Heat another teaspoon of duck fat in the same pan over medium-high heat. Add the bok choy stems, season with salt and pepper, and sauté until browned and seared, about 3 minutes. Transfer to the bowl with the mushrooms.

- Heat another teaspoon of duck fat in the same pan over medium-high heat. Add the onion, season with salt and pepper, and sauté until tender, about 5 minutes. Add the garlic and Thai chilies and sauté about 1 minute more. Add the Lapsang Souchong Rice and sauté until warmed through and softened, then continue sautéing until the rice seems firm again, about 3 minutes.

- Push the rice to the side of the pan, and heat another teaspoon of duck fat or oil in the cleared area. Add the beaten eggs, season with salt and pepper, and cook, stirring, until scrambled and cooked through. Stir into the rice. (If your pan doesn't seem big enough, scramble the eggs in a separate pan.) Add the contents of the bowl, frozen peas and carrots, and the chopped duck. Sauté everything together until warmed through.

- In a small bowl, stir together the plum sauce, soy sauce, hoisin sauce, Chinese vinegar, ginger, and five-spice powder. Drizzle over the rice, stirring until evenly dispersed. Add the bok choy leaves and cook until wilted, about 1 minute.

- Divide rice among plates, garnish with chopped green onions and serve.

Vietnamese Pho Fried Rice with Beef, Cilantro, and Bean Sprouts

Anh Luu is a first-generation Vietnamese chef in Portland (by way of New Orleans) who has a genius way of giving Asian dishes a Mexican twist. Her *phorrito*, which spins the flavors of Vietnam's iconic soup into burrito form, is a cult favorite. I took a page from her book of culinary mash-ups and turned the star-anise-scented classic into much-speedier fried rice. She taught me that the secret to good *pho* is in the charred onion and ginger, because it concentrates the flavors and adds subtle depth. It's definitely worth the extra few minutes.

MAKES 4 SERVINGS

HERB TOPPING
½ cup Thai basil, finely chopped (see note)
½ cup cilantro, finely chopped
½ medium yellow onion, finely chopped

FRIED RICE
1 large yellow onion, skin on, quartered
1 (2-inch) piece fresh ginger, skin on,
   halved lengthwise
2 teaspoons vegetable oil, divided
1 serrano pepper, minced
8 ounces ground pork

8 ounces ground beef (90 percent lean)
2 teaspoons Chinese five-spice powder
1 teaspoon cinnamon
1 teaspoon kosher salt
2 teaspoons fish sauce
1 teaspoon soy sauce
4 cups cold cooked rice
2 cups bean sprouts
Hoisin sauce, for serving
Sriracha, for serving
1 lime, cut into wedges

▪ **TO MAKE THE TOPPING:** In a medium bowl, combine the basil, cilantro, and onion. Set aside.

▪ **TO MAKE THE FRIED RICE:** Adjust the oven rack to 3 to 4 inches from the broiler element, and preheat broiler to high. Place onions and ginger (skin side up) on a baking sheet or broiler pan. Broil until onion is blackened and charred around the edges and ginger looks a bit shriveled and skin is deeply browned. (Alternatively, you can char the onion and ginger on the grill.) When cool enough to handle, cut off just the most burnt, charcoal-like parts of the onion, then dice. Scrape the skin off the ginger and mince.

- Heat 1 teaspoon of the oil in a large sauté pan over medium-high heat. Add the diced onion, ginger, and serrano; sauté until the onions are tender, about 5 minutes. Add the pork and beef and sauté, stirring to break up the meat, until it is no longer pink, 3 to 5 minutes. Add the five-spice powder, cinnamon, salt, fish sauce, and soy sauce. Sauté until evenly distributed. Transfer to a plate.

- Heat the remaining teaspoon of oil, and add the rice. Sauté until warmed through and softened, then continue sautéing until the rice seems firm again, about 3 minutes. Add the bean sprouts and sauté until just beginning to soften, about 1 minute. Add the contents of the plate and cook until heated through. Taste and season with salt.

- Divide the fried rice among plates and sprinkle with the herb topping. Serve with hoisin sauce, sriracha, and lime wedges.

NOTE: Thai basil has stronger, more complex flavors than the ubiquitous Genovese basil. You can tell the difference by its purple stems and a fragrance that's a lot like five-spice powder, with lots of anise and cinnamon notes. Look for it at supermarkets with a wide variety of international ingredients or at Asian markets.

Vietnamese Pork Meatball Banh Mi Fried Rice

Vietnamese sandwiches are a study in mouthwatering contrasts: there's the crispy-soft bun, savory pâté and meat, spicy jalapeño, herby cilantro, and tangy pickled daikon and carrot. One bite makes every taste bud happy. To capture this sandwich perfection in fried rice form, I flavored ground pork with the classic Vietnamese flavors of fish sauce, lemongrass, and sriracha. But it wasn't until I garnished it with the *do chua*, or quick-pickled carrot and daikon, that the dish truly hit my banh mi buttons. Although you can simply sauté all the pork mixture, it's worth the few extra minutes to roll at least half the mixture into tiny meatballs. Not only are they cute, but they also deliver more concentrated flavor.

MAKES 4 SERVINGS

DO CHUA

1 small daikon radish, peeled and cut into matchsticks
1 large carrot, peeled and cut into matchsticks
1 teaspoon kosher salt
1 cup distilled white vinegar
1 cup water
⅓ cup granulated sugar

VIETNAMESE MEATBALLS

1 stalk lemongrass, root end trimmed, outer leaves removed, finely sliced (white part only; about 2 tablespoons)
2 cloves garlic
2 green onions

1 tablespoon fish sauce
1 tablespoon sriracha
1 teaspoon kosher salt
1 pound ground pork

FRIED RICE

1 tablespoon vegetable oil
5 green onions, ends trimmed, cut into 1-inch lengths
4 cups cold cooked rice
1 tablespoon soy sauce
1 tablespoon fish sauce
1 tablespoon sriracha, plus more for serving
½ cup chopped fresh cilantro
1 jalapeño, thinly sliced

▪ **TO MAKE THE DO CHUA:** Combine the daikon and carrot on a colander set in the sink. Sprinkle with salt, and massage the vegetables until they're bendable and have expelled their liquid. In a medium bowl, combine the vinegar, water, and sugar. Stir until the sugar is dissolved. Add the carrot and daikon, pressing to make sure the vegetables are mostly submerged. Cover and refrigerate at least an hour before using, and up to several weeks.

→

- **TO MAKE THE MEATBALLS:** In a food processor, combine the lemongrass, garlic, and green onions. Pulse until finely chopped. Add the fish sauce, sriracha, salt, and pork; pulse until just combined. (Alternatively, you can very finely chop the lemongrass, garlic, and green onions by hand or use a mortar and pestle, then mix with the remaining ingredients.) Roll the meat mixture into heaping teaspoon-size meatballs (alternatively, you can roll just half into meatballs and use a combination of ground pork and meatballs in the fried rice).

- **TO MAKE THE FRIED RICE:** Heat the oil in a large sauté pan over medium-high heat. Add the meatballs and brown on all sides, about 5 minutes. Transfer to a plate. (If you rolled only half the mixture into meatballs, now sauté the ground pork in the pan until cooked through, then transfer to the plate.) Add the green onions and sauté until browned, about 2 minutes. Add the rice and sauté until warmed through and softened, then continue sautéing until the rice seems firm again, about 3 minutes. Add the meatballs and cook until warmed through. In a small bowl, combine the soy sauce, fish sauce, and sriracha. Drizzle the mixture over the rice and stir until evenly coated.

- Divide fried rice among plates and top with do chua (drained), cilantro, and sliced jalapeño.

Pad Thai Fried Rice with Shrimp and Spinach

Turning pad Thai into fried rice is about as simple as swapping out the rice noodles for actual rice. But this dish pushes the flavor envelope a bit with the addition of spicy *sambal oelek*. To make it a more complete meal, I add a few handfuls of spinach or pea shoots for added nutrition.

MAKES 4 SERVINGS

¼ cup tamarind concentrate

3 tablespoons packed dark brown sugar

2 tablespoons fish sauce

1 tablespoon sambal oelek

1 tablespoon plus 1 teaspoon vegetable or extra-virgin olive oil, divided

1 bunch green onions, white and light-green parts cut into 1-inch lengths; dark-green tops thinly sliced and reserved for garnish

4 cups bean sprouts, divided

8 ounces peeled and deveined medium shrimp

2 eggs, beaten

4 cups cold cooked rice

2 cloves garlic, minced

2 cups chopped fresh spinach or pea shoots

⅓ cup chopped fresh cilantro

⅓ cup chopped unsalted roasted peanuts

1 lime, cut into wedges

- In a small bowl, stir together the tamarind concentrate, brown sugar, fish sauce, and sambal oelek. Set aside.

- Heat 1 teaspoon of the oil in a large sauté pan over medium-high heat. Add the 1-inch green onions and 2 cups of the bean sprouts, and sauté until green onions are seared, about 3 minutes. Transfer to a plate.

- Heat another teaspoon of oil, and add the shrimp. Sauté until pink, about 3 minutes. Transfer to the plate with the green onions and sprouts.

$\longrightarrow$

- Add another teaspoon of oil and the beaten egg and cook, stirring, until scrambled. Transfer to the plate.

- Heat the remaining teaspoon of oil and add the rice. Sauté until warmed through and softened, then continue sautéing until the rice seems firm again, about 3 minutes. Add the garlic and cook 1 minute more. Add the spinach or pea shoots and the vegetables, meat, and egg from the plate. Drizzle with the tamarind sauce. Cook, stirring until sauce is evenly distributed and everything is heated through.

- Divide fried rice among plates. Garnish with the remaining bean sprouts, cilantro, and peanuts, and serve with lime wedges on the side.

Nam Khao Tod with Pork Larb

This classic Laotian salad is a carnival of flavors and textures, from the crispy-chewy rice to the sour-salty heat of the dressing. Traditionally, it's made by mixing cooked sticky rice with ingredients like red curry paste, then forming it into balls, like arancini, and deep-frying. The balls are then broken up into a mélange of crispy, chewy, and tender bits and mixed with fermented Thai sausage and a whole host of ingredients. To simplify, I took a page from Farmhouse Kitchen Thai Cuisine, one of my favorite Thai restaurants in Portland, and simply let the curry-seasoned rice dry out before deep-frying it into little clusters. And instead of tracking down the fermented sausage, I make a quick batch of pork *larb*, shot through with spicy chilies, sour lemongrass, lime juice, funky fish sauce, ginger, and garlic. It may not be traditional, but it's incredibly delicious.

MAKES 4 SERVINGS

CURRY RICE CLUSTERS

3 cups cold cooked white rice
1 tablespoon Thai red curry paste
1 tablespoon tomato paste
4 cups vegetable oil, for frying

PORK LARB

1 pound ground pork
3 large cloves garlic, minced
1 (3-inch) piece fresh ginger, peeled and finely grated (2 tablespoons)
1 stalk lemongrass, root end trimmed, outer leaves removed, very finely sliced (white part only; about 2 tablespoons)
2 large shallots, sliced into very thin rounds
2 Thai chilies, or more to taste
5 large napa cabbage leaves, halved lengthwise and thinly sliced crosswise
Zest and juice from 2 limes (¼ cup juice)

2 tablespoons fish sauce
Kosher salt and freshly ground black pepper to taste

SALAD

2 teaspoons Thai roasted red chili paste (*nam prik pao*)
½ cup chopped fresh cilantro, plus more for garnish
½ cup chopped fresh mint, plus more for garnish
Lettuce cups, such as small butter lettuce leaves, hearts of romaine leaves, or endive leaves (optional)

- **TO MAKE THE CURRY RICE CLUSTERS**: Preheat oven to 200 degrees F. In a medium bowl, gently mix together the rice, curry paste, and tomato paste until the rice is evenly coated. Spread the rice on a rimmed baking sheet in an even layer. The rice should be in tiny clusters. Place in the oven and gently bake for 3 to 4 hours, stirring once halfway through. The rice should feel crispy, with a few bendable clusters, and should not be moist on the surface or so dry it's darkened. Remove and keep at room temperature in an airtight container until ready to fry. (Rice can be prepared up to this point several days ahead.)

- Heat the vegetable oil in a deep, 6-quart, heavy-bottomed saucepan until it reaches 400 degrees F. Set a baking sheet lined with several layers of paper towels nearby. Add a handful of rice to the hot oil. Within a second or two, the rice will immediately puff and float to the top. Scoop it out with a fine-mesh skimmer and transfer to the prepared baking sheet. Repeat with the remaining rice. (If the rice doesn't puff up, it's too dry and you'll need to start over. Rice can be fried a couple of hours ahead but is best used the day it's fried.)

- **TO MAKE THE LARB**: Heat a large sauté pan over medium-high heat. Add the pork and sauté, stirring to break up the meat into small pieces, until it is no longer pink, about 5 minutes. Add the garlic, ginger, and lemongrass and sauté for about 1 minute more. Add the shallots and Thai chilies, and sauté until shallots are tender, about 3 minutes. Add the cabbage and sauté until wilted, about 2 minutes.

- In a small bowl, mix together the lime zest, juice, and fish sauce. Drizzle 3 tablespoons of the mixture over the ingredients in the pan and stir until evenly incorporated (reserve the rest to dress the salad). Taste and adjust with more chilies, salt, pepper, or lime juice if desired. Remove from heat and transfer to a large mixing bowl. Allow to cool for a few minutes.

- **TO MAKE THE SALAD**: Stir the red chili paste into the remaining lime juice and fish sauce mixture until fully incorporated.

- Add the curry rice clusters, cilantro, and mint to the bowl with the larb and mix to evenly distribute. Drizzle the lime juice mixture over the top and toss until evenly incorporated.

- Divide the salad among bowls and garnish with more herbs. Serve in lettuce cups if desired.

Thai Fried Coconut Rice with Pork Satay and Spinach

Peanuty satay sauce spiked with coconut, lime, and chilies is so good, I want to dip everything in it, so I had to find a way to turn it into fried rice. But it takes a pantry full of ingredients to make great satay. To streamline the dish without cutting anything out, I created a flavor-packed marinade that does double-duty as the base of the sauce.

MAKES 4 SERVINGS

LIME-CURRY MARINADE

1 shallot

2 cloves garlic

½ cup coconut milk

2 tablespoons Thai red curry paste

2 tablespoons packed dark brown sugar

2 tablespoons fish sauce

2 tablespoons freshly squeezed lime juice

1 tablespoon soy sauce

1 pound pork tenderloin, cut into ¾-inch cubes

LIME-CURRY PEANUT SAUCE

¼ cup smooth natural peanut butter

1 tablespoon water

1 tablespoon coconut milk

⅓ cup reserved marinade

FRIED RICE

2 tablespoons extra-virgin olive oil, plus more if necessary

1 medium yellow onion, diced

1 red bell pepper, diced

2 cloves garlic, minced

4 green onions, ends trimmed, cut into 1-inch lengths

4 cups cold Coconut Rice (see page 43)

2 cups chopped fresh spinach, packed

½ English cucumber, peeled and diced

⅓ cup chopped fresh cilantro

2 Thai chilies (or 1 serrano), minced, or more to taste

1 lime, cut into wedges

Sriracha, for serving

■ **TO MAKE THE MARINADE:** In a food processor or blender, combine the shallot and garlic. Pulse until finely chopped. Add the coconut milk, curry paste, brown sugar, fish sauce, lime juice, and soy sauce. Process until smooth. Transfer ⅓ cup of the marinade to a small bowl to be used in the peanut sauce. Combine the rest of the marinade with the cubed pork in a ziplock bag or medium bowl, mixing until pork is evenly coated. Seal bag or cover bowl and allow to marinate in the refrigerator for at least 1 hour up to overnight.

$\longrightarrow$

- **TO MAKE THE PEANUT SAUCE:** Add the peanut butter, water, and coconut milk to the reserved marinade in the bowl, stirring until combined. Set aside. (Can be made a day ahead and refrigerated.)

- **TO MAKE THE FRIED RICE:** Heat 1 tablespoon of the oil in a large nonstick sauté pan over medium-high heat. Use a slotted spoon to remove the pork from the marinade, shaking the excess off. Add enough of the marinated pork to fill the bottom of the pan without crowding (you may have to sauté in batches). Sauté until browned on both sides, about 3 minutes per side, then transfer to a plate. If browning in batches, scrape out any residue from the bottom of the pan and repeat with the remaining pork, adding more oil if necessary.

- Heat 1½ teaspoons oil in same sauté pan over medium-high heat. Add the onion and bell pepper and sauté until tender-crisp, stirring to scrape up any browned bits from the pork, about 5 minutes. Add the garlic and sauté about 1 minute more. Add the green onions and sauté until lightly browned, stirring occasionally, about 2 minutes.

- Heat the remaining 1½ teaspoons oil in the pan. Add the rice and sauté until warmed through and softened, then continue sautéing until the rice seems firm again, about 3 minutes. Add the pork and cook until heated through. Add the spinach and cook until wilted, about 2 minutes.

- Divide rice among plates and drizzle with the peanut sauce (about 2 tablespoons per bowl). Garnish with cucumbers, cilantro, and chilies. Serve with lime wedges and pass sriracha at the table.

Burmese Fried Rice with Chicken, Herbs, and Crispy Shallots

Bursting with big handfuls of chopped fresh herbs and crispy-crunchy fried shallots, Burmese chicken salad is the perfect summertime dish. It's also a great way to use up leftover roast chicken. Or just poach a couple of chicken breasts. Gently simmered with a couple of smashed garlic cloves, a bay leaf, a big splash of white wine, salt, pepper, and enough water to cover by an inch, and they'll be ready in 10 to 15 minutes.

MAKES 4 SERVINGS

½ cup vegetable or peanut oil

3 shallots, thinly sliced (about 2 cups)

Kosher salt

4 cups cold cooked rice

3 cups chopped or shredded cooked chicken

⅓ cup fresh lime juice

2 tablespoons fish sauce

1¼ cups chopped fresh cilantro

1¼ cups chopped fresh mint

1¼ cups chopped fresh basil

2 Thai chilies, finely minced (or 1 serrano; see note)

½ head napa cabbage, thinly sliced crosswise (about 3 cups)

½ cup roasted unsalted peanuts, chopped

▪ Heat the oil in a medium saucepan over medium heat. Add the shallots and fry until golden, about 10 minutes. Remove with a slotted spoon and drain on a paper-towel-lined plate. Sprinkle with a pinch of salt. Strain the cooking oil through a fine-mesh sieve into a small bowl. (The oil will be infused with shallot flavor; reserve the extra to use in other dishes.)

▪ Heat 1 tablespoon of the shallot cooking oil in a large sauté pan over medium-high heat. Add the rice and sauté until warmed through and softened, then continue sautéing until the rice seems firm again, about 3 minutes. Add the chicken and sauté until heated through. In a small bowl, mix the lime juice and fish sauce together, then pour the mixture over the rice. Sauté until well combined and the liquid is absorbed.

▪ Remove from heat and stir in the herbs, chilies, and cabbage. Divide among plates and garnish with peanuts and shallots.

NOTE: Even if you don't like a lot of spicy heat, don't skip the chilies. They're not too hot, and they're essential to balancing the flavors of the dish.

Nasi Goreng (Indonesian Fried Rice)

The archipelago of islands known as Indonesia is home to hundreds of ethnic groups, which is why the cuisine is some of the most complex in the world, rich with influences from India, the Middle East, China, and Europe. My goal was to capture some of this complexity (without going crazy trying to track down ingredients) in a flavor-packed take on *nasi goreng*. As for each country's fried rice, the ingredients change depending on what's on hand, but a few things set nasi goreng apart—*kecap manis*, which is a sweet, syrupy soy sauce; shrimp paste, which is way funkier than fish sauce; and a hefty hit of chilies. I faithfully built my fried rice on this trio, though I use shrimp paste from a jar rather than the dried brick because it's easier to work with. And as a sort of a shortcut for *basa gede*, the traditional Balinese spice paste, I add Thai red curry paste and sambal oelek to add even more layers of flavor. With these ingredients on hand, a spicy, complex-flavored fried rice can be on the table in minutes.

MAKES 4 SERVINGS

NASI GORENG SAUCE

1 medium shallot, minced

3 large cloves garlic, smashed

2 to 3 Thai chilies, minced

2 teaspoons grated palm sugar or packed dark brown sugar

2 tablespoons kecap manis (see note)

1 tablespoon Thai red curry paste

1 tablespoon sambal oelek

2 teaspoons shrimp paste

FRIED RICE

1 tablespoon plus 2 teaspoons vegetable oil (or more as needed)

8 ounces green beans, cut into 1-inch lengths

8 ounces peeled and deveined medium shrimp

1 boneless, skinless chicken breast (or 2 boneless, skinless chicken thighs), cut into bite-size chunks

4 cups cold cooked rice

3 eggs, beaten

4 green onions, ends trimmed, chopped

Kosher salt

1 cup store-bought fried onions

1 cup cherry tomatoes, halved

½ English cucumber, peeled and diced

1 lime, cut into wedges

- **TO MAKE THE SAUCE:** Pound the shallot, garlic, chilies, and sugar in a mortar and pestle until completely mashed. Stir in the kecap manis, curry paste, sambal oelek, and shrimp paste. (Alternatively, you can puree the ingredients in a small food processor.) Set aside.

- **TO MAKE THE FRIED RICE:** Heat a tablespoon of the oil in a large sauté pan over medium-high heat. Add the green beans and cook until beginning to brown and tender-crisp, about 4 minutes. Transfer to a plate. Add the shrimp to the same pan and sauté over medium-high heat until pink and opaque, 3 to 4 minutes. Transfer to the plate. Add the chicken to the pan (add a little more oil if necessary) and sauté until golden brown, 5 to 6 minutes. Transfer to the plate.

- Heat the remaining teaspoon of oil in the same pan, and add the rice. Sauté over medium-high heat until warmed through and softened, then continue sautéing until the rice seems firm again, about 3 minutes. Push the rice to the side of the pan, and add the remaining teaspoon of oil and the beaten eggs. Cook, stirring, until scrambled and cooked through. (If your pan doesn't seem big enough, scramble the eggs in a separate pan.) Stir into the rice, along with the green onions, and the beans, shrimp, and chicken from the plate. Drizzle the sauce over the rice and sauté until evenly distributed. Taste and season with salt.

- Divide the rice among plates and top with fried onions. Serve with cherry tomatoes, cucumbers, and lime wedges.

NOTE· If you can't find kecap manis, you can make your own: Combine ¼ cup soy sauce and ¼ cup packed dark brown sugar in a small saucepan. Simmer over medium heat until thick and syrupy, 5 to 10 minutes.

Korean Kimchi and Bulgogi Fried Rice

Fried rice with a healthy handful of spicy-funky kimchi is a match made in heaven. But I wanted to pack in even more Korean flavor by adding the gingery goodness of *bulgogi* beef. The marinade is crazy flavorful yet super simple to make, and after the meat is done taking its flavor bath, I reduce the marinade down to a thickened sauce and use it to season the fried rice. If you're not in the mood for meat, mix up the marinade directly in a small saucepan and reduce it. Then top the fried rice with fried eggs.

MAKES 4 SERVINGS

⅓ cup low-sodium soy sauce

3 tablespoons packed dark brown sugar

3 large cloves garlic, minced

1 (2-inch) piece fresh ginger, peeled and grated (1 tablespoon)

1 tablespoon sesame oil

1 tablespoon mirin

1 tablespoon *gochujang*

1 pound flank steak, thinly sliced across the grain and cut into 2-inch pieces

2 tablespoons vegetable oil, divided

Kosher salt

4 green onions, ends trimmed, cut into 1-inch lengths

1 medium yellow onion, diced

4 cups cold cooked rice

1 cup chopped kimchi

½ cup chopped fresh cilantro

2 tablespoons toasted sesame seeds

▪ In a medium bowl, combine the soy sauce, sugar, garlic, ginger, sesame oil, mirin, and gochujang. Add the sliced beef and toss to coat. Cover and allow to marinate in the refrigerator at least 1 hour or up to overnight.

▪ Heat 1 tablespoon of the oil in a large sauté pan over medium-high heat. Use a slotted spoon to remove about half the meat from the marinade, allowing the excess to drip off, and arrange in an even layer in the bottom of the pan without crowding (it's important to give the meat room to cook so it browns and crisps at the edges instead of steaming). Season with salt and allow to cook until seared, 2 to 3 minutes. Turn over and sear the other side until browned, about 3 minutes more. Transfer to a plate and repeat with the remaining meat, adding 2 teaspoons more oil as necessary. Transfer all the meat to the plate.

- Pour the leftover marinade into the pan and bring to a simmer over medium heat. Cook, stirring to scrape up the browned bits, until thickened and reduced to about ¼ cup, 5 to 10 minutes, lowering the heat if necessary so it doesn't burn. Transfer to a small measuring cup or bowl.

- Wipe out the pan, and heat the remaining teaspoon of oil. Add the green onions and sauté until browned and seared, about 3 minutes. Transfer to the plate with the beef. Add the onion and sauté until tender, about 5 minutes. Add the rice and sauté until warmed through and softened; then continue sautéing until the rice seems firm again, about 3 minutes. Add the chopped kimchi, beef, and green onions. Drizzle with about 2 tablespoons of the reduced marinade. Cook, stirring until fully combined and heated through.

- Divide fried rice among bowls and top with cilantro and sesame seeds. Drizzle with more marinade if desired.

Filipino Fried Rice (Sinangag) with Adobo Chicken

A big hit of garlic is what really makes Filipino fried rice different from any others. But this version pairs it with that country's other iconic dish: adobo chicken. The gingery, sweet-and-sour marinade tenderizes the chicken and makes it downright irresistible. The marinade is so good, I boil it down and use it to flavor the fried rice too.

MAKES 4 SERVINGS

ADOBO CHICKEN

½ cup distilled white vinegar

¼ cup low-sodium soy sauce

3 cloves garlic, minced

1 (2-inch) piece fresh ginger, peeled and grated (1 tablespoon)

1 tablespoon packed dark brown sugar

2 tablespoons vegetable oil, plus more as needed, divided

1 teaspoon freshly ground black pepper

4 boneless, skinless chicken thighs, cut into bite-size chunks

FRIED RICE

1 tablespoon vegetable oil, divided

4 green onions, ends trimmed, cut into 1-inch lengths

3 small baby bok choy, thinly sliced cross-wise, with the stems kept separate

1 medium yellow onion, diced

4 cloves garlic, minced

4 cups cold cooked rice

2 eggs, beaten

Kosher salt and freshly ground black pepper

1 cup frozen peas and carrots

▪ **TO MAKE THE ADOBO CHICKEN:** In a large ziplock bag or medium bowl, combine the vinegar, soy sauce, garlic, ginger, brown sugar, 1 tablespoon of the oil, and pepper. Add the chicken, toss to coat, and seal or cover. Allow to marinate in the refrigerator for at least 1 hour but no more than 4 hours. (Because of the large amount of vinegar in the marinade, the meat can have a mealy texture if left in the marinade too long.)

▪ Heat another tablespoon of the oil in a large sauté pan over medium-high heat. Use a slotted spoon to remove about half the chicken from the marinade, allowing the excess to drip off, and arrange in an even layer in the bottom of the pan without crowding (it's important to give the meat room to cook so it browns and crisps at the edges instead of steaming). Sauté until golden brown and cooked through, 2 to 3 minutes per side. Transfer to a plate and repeat with the remaining meat, adding more oil as necessary. Transfer all the chicken to the plate.

▪ Pour the leftover marinade into the same sauté pan and bring to a simmer over medium heat, stirring to scrape up the browned bits. Simmer until liquid is thickened and reduced to about ⅓ cup, about 8 minutes, lowering the heat if necessary so it doesn't burn. Transfer to a small measuring cup or bowl.

▪ **TO MAKE THE FRIED RICE:** Wipe out the sauté pan and set over medium-high heat. Add 1 teaspoon of the oil, the green onions, and bok choy stems. Sauté until browned and seared, about 3 minutes. Transfer to the plate with the chicken. Add another teaspoon of oil to the same pan and add the onion. Sauté over medium-high heat until tender, about 5 minutes. Add the garlic and sauté about 1 minute more. Add the rice and sauté until warmed through and softened, then continue sautéing until the rice seems firm again, about 3 minutes. Drizzle with 3 tablespoons of the reduced marinade and toss until evenly mixed.

▪ Push the rice to the side of the pan, and add the remaining teaspoon of oil into the cleared area. Add the beaten eggs, season with a sprinkle of salt and pepper, and cook, stirring, until scrambled and cooked through. (If your pan doesn't seem big enough, scramble the eggs in a separate pan.) Stir into the rice. Add the sliced bok choy leaves, frozen peas and carrots, and the contents of the plate. Cook, stirring until fully combined and heated through Taste and season with more salt if desired.

▪ Divide rice among plates and garnish with a drizzle of the reduced marinade.

Flavors of India, Africa, and the Middle East

⁄⁀\⁊⁄ ⁊⁄⁀\⁊⁄ ⁊⁄⁀\⁊⁄ ⁊⁄⁀\⁊⁄ ⁊⁄⁀\⁊⁄ ⁊⁄⁀\⁊⁄ ⁊⁄⁀\⁊⁄ ⁊⁄⁀\⁊⁄

Rice is just as important in this part of the world as it is in the Far East, though here the variety of choice is usually long-grain basmati. Rice here gets an entirely different treatment too. Instead of serving as a blank backdrop, it often stands on its own as a side dish, all dressed up with a variety of spices and aromatics specifically chosen to accent a particular meal. In this section, the wealth of warm spices that define Indian, African, and Middle Eastern cuisines are used to flavor a range of fried rice dishes. They may not always be traditional, but they're definitely delicious.

⁄⁀\⁊⁄ ⁊⁄⁀\⁊⁄ ⁊⁄⁀\⁊⁄ ⁊⁄⁀\⁊⁄ ⁊⁄⁀\⁊⁄ ⁊⁄⁀\⁊⁄ ⁊⁄⁀\⁊⁄ ⁊⁄⁀\⁊⁄

Vagharelo Bhaat (Gujarati Fried Rice) with Chicken and Cilantro Yogurt

Every region of India has its own version of fried rice, which is often called "tempered" rice because it's flavored with spices cooked in oil. This version takes its inspiration from the Gujarat region, where mustard seeds, chili powder, and garam masala are typically used. Although many Gujaratis are vegetarian, I add chicken thighs to make it a full meal. Crunchy peanuts add even more protein, and a lashing of cilantro yogurt gives it a bright, creamy richness that tempers the heat from the chili powder.

MAKES 4 SERVINGS

2 tablespoons vegetable oil, divided
½ cup roasted unsalted peanuts
1 pound boneless, skinless chicken thighs, cut into bite-size pieces
Kosher salt and freshly ground black pepper
1 tablespoon black or brown mustard seeds
1 medium yellow onion, diced
1½ teaspoons garam masala
1 teaspoon ground cumin
1 teaspoon ground turmeric

½ teaspoon Indian red chili powder (or cayenne)
3 cloves garlic, minced
4 cups cold cooked basmati rice
1½ cups frozen peas and carrots
Zest of 1 lemon
2 tablespoons freshly squeezed lemon juice
⅓ cup chopped fresh cilantro
½ cup plain whole milk Greek yogurt
¼ teaspoon kosher salt

- Heat 1 tablespoon of the oil in a large sauté pan over medium-high heat. Add the peanuts and sauté until they look and smell toasted, about 2 minutes. Transfer to a medium bowl. (I like the texture of peanut halves, but if you want smaller pieces, roughly chop.)

- Heat 2 teaspoons of the oil in the sauté pan over medium-high heat. Add the chicken in an even layer (you may have to sauté in batches), season with salt and pepper, and sauté until browned and cooked through, about 5 minutes. Transfer to the bowl with the nuts.

$\longrightarrow$

- Heat the remaining teaspoon of oil in the pan over medium-high heat. Add the mustard seeds and allow to toast for a few seconds until they start to pop (you may want to use a splatter screen to keep them from launching out of the pan). Add the onion and sauté until tender, about 5 minutes. Add the garam masala, cumin, turmeric, chili powder, and garlic and sauté 1 minute more. Add the rice and sauté until warmed through and softened, then continue sautéing until the rice seems firm again (if necessary, add a squeeze of lemon or splash of water to help the spices to evenly distribute). Add the peas and carrots and cook until warmed through.

- Add the chicken, peanuts, and lemon zest, stirring until evenly incorporated. Drizzle the rice with lemon juice and season to taste with salt and pepper.

- In a small bowl, combine cilantro, yogurt, salt, and a few grinds of black pepper. Divide the fried rice among bowls and top with the cilantro yogurt.

Chitranna (Indian Lemon Rice) with Curry Leaves and Cashews

This fried rice hails from southern India, where it's spiked with lemon, spicy chilies, and fresh curry leaves that add a deep, fragrant, herbal flavor. *Chitranna* is also often made with a teaspoon or so of dried *urad dal* which adds a nutty note. But since it's hard to find and such a small amount, I skip it and add a few extra cashews instead. You can make this with the Lemon Rice on page 42, or just add an extra tablespoon of lemon juice when serving.

MAKES 4 SERVINGS

2 tablespoons vegetable oil, divided

½ cup raw cashews or unsalted roasted peanuts

1 pound boneless, skinless chicken thighs, cut into bite-size pieces

Kosher salt and freshly ground black pepper

1 tablespoon black or brown mustard seeds

1 teaspoon cumin seeds

1 serrano pepper, minced

15 fresh curry leaves (see note)

1 medium yellow onion, diced

3 cloves garlic, minced

1 teaspoon ground turmeric

4 cups cold cooked Lemon Rice (page 42) or basmati rice

3 cups chopped fresh baby spinach

Zest of 1 lemon

1 to 2 tablespoons freshly squeezed lemon juice

- Heat 1 tablespoon of the oil in a large sauté pan over medium-high heat. Add the cashews and sauté until they look and smell toasted, about 5 minutes (or 2 minutes for peanuts). Transfer to medium bowl. (I like the texture of whole nuts, but if you want smaller pieces, roughly chop.)

- Heat 2 teaspoons of the oil in the sauté pan over medium-high heat. Add the chicken in an even layer (you may have to sauté in batches), season with salt and pepper, and sauté until browned and cooked through, about 5 minutes. Transfer to the bowl with the nuts.

$\longrightarrow$

- Heat the remaining teaspoon of oil in the sauté pan, and add the mustard seeds, and then the cumin seeds just a few seconds later. Allow to toast for a few seconds until the seeds start to pop (you may want to use a splatter screen to keep them from launching out of the pan). Add the serrano and curry leaves. Sauté for about 30 seconds to wilt the curry leaves, then add the onion and sauté until tender, about 5 minutes. Add the garlic and turmeric and sauté 1 minute more. Add the rice and sauté until warmed through and softened, then continue sautéing until the rice seems firm again, about 3 minutes. Add the spinach and cook until wilted, about 3 minutes.

- Add the chicken, cashews, and lemon zest, stirring until evenly incorporated. Drizzle the rice with lemon juice and season to taste with more salt and pepper.

NOTE: Fresh curry leaves are usually available at Asian, Indian, and even some Middle Eastern markets.

Jollof Fried Rice with Chakalaka

One of the most iconic and comforting dishes from West Africa, *jollof* rice is essentially a one-pot dish of rice cooked in a spicy tomato stew. Everyone loves it, even if they don't always agree on how to make it. Depending on which country they're from, and even which family, cooks will change up the meat, the vegetables, the spices, even the technique. This recipe captures the spirit and flavors of the deeply tomatoey dish, but allows you to use leftover rice instead. To brighten it up, I add a big scoop of sweet savory *chakalaka,* an addictive relish of tomatoes, onions, peppers, and baked beans. Since the base of chakalaka and jollof are so similar, I streamline the prep work by making a big batch of the sautéed vegetables, then using half for the relish and half for the rice.

MAKES 4 SERVINGS

2 tablespoons vegetable oil, divided

1 medium yellow onion, diced

1 green bell pepper, diced

1 habanero pepper, minced

1 jalapeño pepper, minced

4 large cloves garlic, minced

1 (3-inch) piece fresh ginger, peeled and minced (1½ tablespoons)

¼ head red, green, or napa cabbage, core removed, halved lengthwise, and thinly sliced crosswise (2 cups)

1 large carrot, peeled and grated (1 cup)

2 Roma tomatoes or 1 medium slicing tomato, diced

2 teaspoons curry powder (preferably from an African market)

1½ teaspoon smoked paprika

1 teaspoon kosher salt

1 (13-ounce) can baked beans, drained (½ cup beans)

Kosher salt and freshly ground black pepper

1 pound ground beef (90 percent lean)

4 cups cold cooked Tomato Rice (page 44; see note)

→

- Heat 2 teaspoons of oil in a large sauté pan over medium-high heat. Add the onion, green pepper, habanero, and jalapeño. Sauté until tender, about 7 minutes. Add the garlic and ginger and sauté 1 minute more. Add another teaspoon of oil if necessary, then add the cabbage, carrots, and tomatoes. Sauté until cabbage is wilted, about 5 minutes. Season with the curry powder, smoked paprika, and salt and pepper to taste. Transfer 4 cups of the mixture to a medium bowl and set aside.

- Add the drained baked beans to the mixture in the pan and sauté until heated through to make the chakalaka. Taste and season with salt and pepper. Transfer to a small serving bowl. Wash and dry the pan.

- Heat 2 teaspoons of the oil in the sauté pan over medium-high heat. Add the ground beef and cook until no longer pink, about 5 minutes. Transfer to the medium bowl with the sautéed vegetables.

- Heat the remaining teaspoon of oil in the sauté pan over medium-high heat. Add the rice and sauté until warmed through and softened, then continue sautéing until the rice seems firm again, about 3 minutes. Add the vegetables and meat from the bowl and sauté, stirring, until evenly distributed and ingredients are warmed through. Season with salt to taste.

- Divide the rice among bowls and serve topped with a generous scoop of chakalaka.

NOTE: If you don't have Tomato Rice on hand, you can use cold cooked white rice and add ¼ cup of tomato paste when sautéing the rice.

Mujadara Fried Rice

Just lentils, rice, and caramelized onions, *mujadara* is so simple, cheap, and comforting, it's no wonder it's commonly found from home kitchens to street vendors all over the Middle East. Built on pantry staples, it's one of those go-to one-pot dishes you can always turn to when the fridge is bare but it's also accommodating to whatever leftover proteins and vegetables you might want to tuck in. Traditionally, the rice and lentils for mujadara are cooked together into a kind of pilaf, but this recipe gives it a fried rice twist. I kept it vegetarian, adding spinach and a lashing of Greek yogurt to make it a more complete meal, but ground beef or lamb sautéed with a little more Middle Eastern Spice Mix (page 52) would be an excellent addition. A tub of fried onions from the Asian market is an easy way to add even more oniony flavor and much-appreciated crunch.

MAKES 4 SERVINGS

LENTILS

8 ounces (1 cup) dry green lentils, rinsed and sorted
2 cups broth (vegetable or chicken)
2 cloves garlic, smashed
1 bay leaf

FRIED RICE

1 tablespoon extra virgin olive oil
1 tablespoon unsalted butter
2 medium yellow onions, halved and thinly sliced
2 teaspoons kosher salt, divided

3 large cloves garlic, minced
1 tablespoon plus 1 teaspoon Middle Eastern Spice Mix (see page 52)
1 teaspoon ground cumin
1 teaspoon ground coriander
3 cups cold cooked basmati rice
4 ounces (3 cups) chopped fresh spinach
1 cup store-bought fried onions
1 cup plain whole milk Greek yogurt, or *labneh* (optional)
½ cup chopped fresh Italian parsley

TO MAKE THE LENTILS: Combine lentils, broth, garlic, and bay leaf in a medium saucepan over medium-high heat. Cover, bring to a boil, reduce to a bare simmer, and cook until tender, 15 to 20 minutes. Transfer to a colander set in the sink and allow excess liquid to drain. You should have about 2½ cups of lentils.

→

- **TO MAKE THE FRIED RICE:** Heat the oil and butter in a large sauté pan over medium-high heat. When butter melts, add the sliced onions, season with 1 teaspoon of the salt, and sauté, stirring occasionally, until most are brown around the edges, about 8 minutes. Reduce heat to medium-low and continue cooking, stirring occasionally, until onions are deep brown and very soft, 10 to 15 more minutes.

- Add the garlic, increase heat to medium-high, and cook until fragrant, about 1 minute. Stir in the remaining 1 teaspoon salt, along with the spice mix, cumin, and coriander. Add the cold cooked rice and sauté until heated through and completely mixed with the spices and onions. Add the cooked lentils and chopped spinach, and cook until lentils are heated through and spinach is wilted, about 2 minutes.

- Divide mixture among plates and top with crunchy onions, yogurt, and parsley.

KOSHARI VARIATION: *Koshari* is the national dish of Egypt and almost identical to mujadara except for the addition of macaroni and chickpeas, which add a really fun texture, and the garnish of spicy-tomatoey *shatta* sauce. To make it, add 2 cups of cooked elbow macaroni and 1 cup of drained and rinsed chickpeas along with the lentils. Serve topped with Shatta Sauce (page 52).

Fried Cauliflower Rice with Turkey Kofta, Mint, and Feta

The spice trio of cumin, coriander, and cinnamon is the cornerstone of a whole category of Middle Eastern ground meat dishes called *kofta*. Here I use the spices to enrich a lean and healthy fried rice built on turkey and riced cauliflower, which are just tiny pieces of raw cauliflower you can find in bags In the produce section or frozen foods aisle. This dish is so richly flavored, you'd never know it's so good for you.

MAKES 4 SERVINGS

1 tablespoon unsalted butter

⅓ cup pine nuts

1 tablespoon plus 1 teaspoon extra-virgin olive oil, divided

1 green bell pepper, diced

1 medium yellow onion, diced

3 garlic cloves, minced

1 pound ground turkey

1 tablespoon plus 1 teaspoon ground cumin

1 tablespoon plus 1 teaspoon ground coriander

1½ teaspoons kosher salt

1 teaspoon ground cinnamon

½ teaspoon freshly ground black pepper

½ teaspoon ground cayenne pepper

4 cups cauliflower rice (or cooked and cooled rice, or a combination of both)

1 cup chopped fresh cilantro

½ cup chopped fresh mint leaves

3 ounces (¾ cup) feta cheese, crumbled

- Melt the butter in a large sauté pan over medium-low heat. Add the pine nuts and gently sauté until golden brown, about 5 minutes. Transfer to a small bowl.

- Heat 2 teaspoons of the oil in the same sauté pan over medium-high heat. Add the bell pepper and onion and sauté until tender, about 5 minutes. Add the garlic and sauté a minute more. Add the turkey, cumin, coriander, salt, cinnamon, pepper, and cayenne. Cook, breaking up the meat, until cooked through, about 5 minutes. Transfer to a medium bowl.

- Heat the remaining 2 teaspoons of oil in the same sauté pan over medium-high heat. Add the cauliflower rice and sauté, stirring only occasionally, until just beginning to brown, about 10 minutes. Add the meat mixture back to the pan. Remove from heat and stir in the cilantro and mint.

- Divide mixture among plates. Serve topped with crumbled feta and the toasted pine nuts.

Moroccan Fried Rice with Chicken, Saffron, and Figs

One bite of a tagine and you'll see why Moroccan cuisine is known for its mastery of savory and sweet. The meaty stews are gently sweetened with dried fruits and warm spices like cinnamon and ginger, resulting in a rich yet balanced dish that hits all your cravings at once. They're usually served with couscous, but here I took the principle of tagine plus starch and turned it into an easy fried rice. If you don't have time to make the preserved lemon, just buy it. Its bright, salty bitterness is essential to balancing the dish's flavors. If you don't have a Middle Eastern market near you, check the olive bar or international foods aisle at well-stocked supermarkets like Whole Foods.

MAKES 4 SERVINGS

1 tablespoon extra-virgin olive oil, plus more as needed

1 pound boneless, skinless chicken thighs, cut into ½-inch pieces

2 teaspoons kosher salt, divided

1 teaspoon freshly ground black pepper, divided

1 large yellow onion, diced

3 large cloves garlic, minced

1½ teaspoons ground cumin

1½ teaspoons ground coriander

½ teaspoon ground ginger

¼ teaspoon ground cinnamon

¼ teaspoon ground allspice

⅛ teaspoon ground cloves

4 cups cold cooked basmati rice

Pinch of saffron threads, ground and dissolved into ¼ cup hot water (see note)

⅓ cup finely diced dried Mission figs

¼ Preserved Lemon (page 51), finely diced (skin and flesh)

¼ cup finely diced dried apricots or cherries (optional)

⅓ cup toasted pine nuts, slivered almonds, or chopped roasted unsalted pistachios (see note)

⅓ cup chopped fresh cilantro

▪ Heat the oil in a large sauté pan over medium-high heat. Add the chicken in an even layer without crowding, sprinkle with 1 teaspoon of the salt and ½ teaspoon of the pepper, and sear until browned on one side, about 3 minutes. Turn the pieces over and brown on the other side, about 3 minutes more. (If your pan isn't big enough to arrange the chicken without crowding, brown it in batches. Otherwise, it will steam instead of brown.) Transfer chicken to a plate.

- Add the onion to the pan and sauté until tender, stirring to scrape up the browned bits at the bottom of the pan, about 5 minutes. (Add a little more oil to the pan if the onions seem to be sticking.) Add the garlic and sauté until fragrant, about 1 minute more. Add the cumin, coriander, ginger, cinnamon, allspice, cloves, remaining salt, and remaining pepper. Stir to mix evenly.

- Add the cold rice to the pan and sauté, stirring to scrape up any bits at the bottom of the pan, until rice is evenly mixed. Pour the saffron water on top and continue to sauté until rice is heated through.

- Add the chicken to the rice mixture, along with the figs, preserved lemon, and apricots. Sauté until heated through. Divide among plates and serve topped with the pine nuts and cilantro.

NOTE: If your saffron is too moist to crumble easily, lightly toast it in a dry pan over medium heat for about 1 minute (or microwave on a plate for about 1 minute). When it cools, it should be brittle enough to crumble. Crush it in a mortar and pestle or between two spoons.

To toast pine nuts or slivered almonds, melt 1 tablespoon of unsalted butter in a sauté pan over medium-low heat. Add the nuts and gently sauté until browned, about 5 minutes. Transfer to a small bowl.

Fried Rice with Halloumi, Pickled Onions, and Zhug

I'm always looking for excuses to fry more *halloumi*. The salty, springy, semisoft cheese is magically grillable, with the outside getting crispy-toasty and the inside deliciously melted. Traditionally made with goat and sheep milk, it's quite rich, so I pair it with Israeli *zhug*, a spicy herbal pesto of sorts, and tangy pickled onions. You can take a shortcut and buy premade zhug—even Trader Joe's now sells tubs of it near the hummus. The pickled onions add bright flavor, color, and crunch, and they're great on sandwiches and grain salads. But if you want to skip that step too, this dish will still be delicious.

MAKES 4 SERVINGS

PICKLED ONIONS

2 teaspoons cumin seeds
2 teaspoons coriander seeds
½ cup red wine vinegar
¼ cup water
1 red onion, halved and thinly sliced
2 cloves garlic, smashed
2 tablespoons granulated sugar
1 tablespoon kosher salt

ZHUG

2 green cardamom pods, seeds only
1 teaspoon black peppercorns
1 teaspoon coriander seeds
¼ teaspoon cumin seeds
1 serrano pepper (remove the seeds if you don't like heat)
2 cloves garlic
½ cup fresh Italian parsley
½ cup fresh cilantro
¼ cup extra-virgin olive oil
1 tablespoon plus 1 teaspoon freshly squeezed lemon juice
Kosher salt

FRIED RICE

3 tablespoons extra-virgin olive oil, divided
⅓ cup pine nuts
3 small Japanese eggplant, cut into ½-inch thick rounds
Kosher salt and freshly ground black pepper
1 medium zucchini, cut into quarters lengthwise, then crosswise into ½-inch pieces
8 ounces halloumi, cut into ½-inch-thick slabs
1 large yellow onion, diced
3 large cloves garlic, minced
2 cups cauliflower rice
2 cups cold cooked basmati rice
1 tablespoon sherry vinegar
1 cup plain whole milk Greek yogurt, or 1 lemon, cut into wedges

$\longrightarrow$

- **TO MAKE THE PICKLED ONIONS:** Set a medium saucepan over medium-high heat. Add the cumin and coriander seeds. Allow to toast until fragrant and just beginning to darken, about 2 minutes. Add the vinegar, water, onions, garlic, sugar, and salt. Bring to a simmer. Cook until the sugar dissolves and onions have begun to wilt and give off some of their color, about 2 minutes. Remove from heat and allow to completely cool. Cover and refrigerate until ready to use. (Onions will keep refrigerated for several weeks.)

- **TO MAKE THE ZHUG:** Heat a small sauté pan over medium-high heat. Add the seeds from the cardamom pods, peppercorns, coriander seeds, and cumin seeds. Allow to toast until fragrant and just beginning to darken, about 1 minute. Remove from heat and transfer to a food processor or blender. Add the serrano, garlic, parsley, and cilantro. Pulse until finely chopped. Add the olive oil and lemon juice; pulse until combined. Season with salt to taste. Cover and refrigerate until ready to use. (Zhug can be made up to 1 week ahead.)

- **TO MAKE THE FRIED RICE:** Heat 1 tablespoon of the olive oil in a large sauté pan set over medium-high heat. Add the pine nuts and gently sauté until browned, about 5 minutes. Transfer to a small bowl.

- Heat another tablespoon of the oil in the same sauté pan, and add the eggplant. Season with salt and pepper and allow to sear until browned, about 3 minutes. Turn over and sear the other side until browned, about 3 minutes more. Transfer to a medium bowl.

- Heat 2 teaspoons of the oil in the same sauté pan. Add the zucchini, season with salt and pepper, and sear until browned, 2 to 3 minutes per side. Transfer to the bowl with the eggplant.

- Add the halloumi to the same pan and sear until brown, about 2 minutes. Turn and cook the other side until seared. Transfer to a cutting board and allow to cool a bit before cutting into bite-size pieces.

- Heat the remaining teaspoon of oil in the same sauté pan. Add the onion, season with salt and pepper, and sauté until tender, about 5 minutes. Add the garlic and sauté about 1 minute more. Add the cauliflower rice and cold basmati rice to the pan and sauté until warmed through and beginning to take on a little color, about 3 minutes. Stir in the sherry vinegar and 3 tablespoons of the zhug until evenly incorporated. Add the vegetables, halloumi, and pine nuts back to the pan and sauté until warmed through. Season with salt and pepper to taste.

- In a small bowl, mix the yogurt with 2 tablespoons of zhug. Divide fried rice among plates. Top each with about ¼ cup yogurt sauce, a generous spoonful of zhug, and pickled onions.

Lubia Polow (Persian Green Bean Rice with Beef)

OK, so technically this isn't typical fried rice, but I think the Persian technique of cooking rice to form a crusty *tahdig* is in the spirit of fried rice. Think about it: it uses precooked rice and a good glug of oil. Besides, it's flat-out delicious. What I love about *lubia polow* is it includes both a vegetable and protein, making it a full-on dinner, especially if you serve it with a tossed green salad. Don't be intimidated by the multitude of steps involved in ensuring you get a crispy tahdig. It's not hard, and after doing it once, it won't seem so mysterious the next time.

MAKES 6 SERVINGS

2 cups uncooked basmati rice, rinsed in several changes of water

2 tablespoons kosher salt (for the cooking liquid)

2 teaspoons extra-virgin olive oil

8 ounces green beans, ends trimmed, cut into thirds

1 medium yellow onion, diced

4 cloves garlic, minced

1 pound ground beef (90 percent lean) or lamb (or a combination of both)

¼ cup tomato paste

1 tablespoon plus 1 teaspoon Middle Eastern Spice Mix (page 52), divided

Kosher salt and freshly ground black pepper

⅓ cup plain whole milk Greek yogurt

½ teaspoon kosher salt

3 tablespoons unsalted butter or oil

Pinch of saffron threads, ground and dissolved in ¼ cup hot water (see note)

▪ Bring a large pot of water to a boil and add the rice and salt. Boil for 3 to 5 minutes, until soft but still hard in the very center (it will finish cooking later). Drain through a fine-mesh sieve set in the sink and rinse with cold water to stop the cooking. Set aside. (Rice can be prepared several hours ahead.)

▪ Heat the oil in a large sauté pan over medium-high heat. Add the green beans and sauté, stirring only occasionally, until seared and browned, about 5 minutes. Transfer to a medium bowl.

$\longrightarrow$

- Add the onions to the same sauté pan and sauté until tender, about 5 minutes. Add the garlic and sauté about 1 minute more. Add the meat and sauté, stirring to break up, until no longer pink, about 3 minutes. (If the meat has released a great deal of fat, pour it off into a small bowl and discard when cool.)

- Push the ingredients to the side of the pan, and add the tomato paste to the cleared area. Cook until slightly darkened and thicker, about 2 minutes. Stir the tomato paste into the rest of the ingredients in the pan, then add the green beans back to the pan. Add 1 tablespoon of the spice mix and season with salt and pepper to taste. Remove from heat.

- In a small bowl, make the tahdig mixture by combining 1 cup of the cooked rice with the yogurt, ½ teaspoon of salt, and the remaining 1 teaspoon of spice mix.

- Heat the butter or oil in a 6-quart Dutch oven (nonstick or enameled cast-iron) over medium heat, turning to evenly coat the bottom and partway up the sides. Spread the rice-yogurt mixture across the bottom and 1½ inches up the sides of the pot. Add the remaining rice and the beef mixture in layers, starting with one-third of the rice, then half of the beef mixture, another third of rice, the remaining beef mixture, and then the rest of the rice. Aim to shape it in a pyramid, which helps steam escape up the sides of the pot. Drizzle the saffron water over the top. Use the handle of a wooden spoon to make several holes all the way down to the bottom of the pot, which will further help steam escape and form the crispy crust. Cover the pot with a clean dish cloth (folded so that the edges don't hang too close to the burner), and set the lid on top. Allow to cook for 10 minutes over medium-high heat.

- Reduce heat to medium-low, and set a heat diffuser between the burner and the pot. (If you don't have a diffuser, invert a metal pie dish over the burner to act as a diffuser. If you don't have either one, you will need to turn the pot a quarter turn every 10 minutes or so to ensure the crust cooks evenly.) Allow to cook on medium-low for 45 minutes, until a brown crust of rice has formed on the bottom.

• Take the pot off the heat and remove the lid, taking care not to let condensation on the underside fall in. Scoop some of the rice out onto a serving platter, then gently remove the tahdig with a spatula and set on top (alternatively, if you're strong and careful, you can invert the whole pot onto a serving platter, but the pot will be hot and heavy). Pass the platter of rice with the browned tahdig at the table, allowing everyone to get a scoop of each. Serve with a crispy green salad.

NOTE: If your saffron is too moist to crumble easily, lightly toast it in a dry pan over medium heat for about 1 minute (or microwave on a plate for about 1 minute). When it cools, it should be brittle enough to crumble. Crush it in a mortar and pestle or between two spoons.

Cruising through Europe and the Mediterranean

//\ \\/ //\ \\/ //\ \\/ //\ \\/ //\ \\/ //\ \\/ //\ \\/ //\ \\/

The countries of the Mediterranean certainly have their rice
traditions, most famously risotto and paella, but generally
speaking, rice isn't a cornerstone of European cuisine. That's
not to say, however, that starches don't play a huge role; they
just take a different form. Take out the pasta, bread, potatoes,
and dumplings from Europe's traditional dishes, and they're
unrecognizable. But if you swap them with rice? Well, now you've
hit the sweet spot between familiar and far-out.

//\ \\/ //\ \\/ //\ \\/ //\ \\/ //\ \\/ //\ \\/ //\ \\/ //\ \\/

Leek and Wild Mushroom Fried Rice

The quintessentially northern European combination of leeks and mushrooms is delicious any time of the year. Generally I reach for king trumpet, shiitake, and oyster mushrooms, though even ubiquitous creminis would work too. And to deepen the dish's savory umami notes, add a dash of Bragg's amino acids and a sprinkle of real truffle salt. The Bragg's is cheap, but the salt is pricey. Find a little room in your budget for it, and you'll find yourself sprinkling it on everything, even popcorn.

MAKES 4 SERVINGS

2 tablespoons unsalted butter, divided
2 tablespoons extra-virgin olive oil, divided
12 ounces mixed wild mushrooms, such as
   king trumpet, shiitake, and oyster, roughly
   chopped
Kosher salt and freshly ground black pepper
1 large leek, white and light-green parts
   halved lengthwise and thinly sliced
   crosswise

4 cloves garlic, minced
1 tablespoon chopped fresh thyme, divided
4 cups cold cooked rice
2 teaspoons Bragg Liquid Aminos
2 teaspoons rice vinegar
Truffle salt or porcini salt (optional)
½ cup shredded gruyère cheese
½ cup chopped roasted hazelnuts
½ cup chopped fresh chives

▪ Heat 1 tablespoon of the butter and 1 tablespoon of the oil in a large sauté pan over medium-high heat. Add the mushrooms in an even layer without crowding, season with salt and pepper, and sauté until browned, about 5 minutes. (Sauté the mushrooms in batches if they won't all fit in the pan, adding more oil and/or butter as necessary. Otherwise they'll steam instead of sear.) Transfer to a plate.

▪ Heat the remaining tablespoon of butter and oil in the pan over medium-high heat, and add the leeks. Season with salt and pepper. Sauté until soft, about 5 minutes. Add the garlic and sauté 1 minute more. Add the rice and 2 teaspoons of the thyme. Sauté until rice is warmed through and softened, then continue sautéing until the rice seems firm again, about 3 minutes. Season with Bragg's and rice vinegar and stir until evenly distributed.

▪ Add the mushrooms back to the pan and cook until heated through. Season with truffle or porcini salt, or adjust with more kosher salt. Divide rice among plates, garnish generously with gruyère, hazelnuts, chives, and the remaining teaspoon of thyme.

Salmon and Asparagus Fried Rice with Lemon and Fresh Dill

Maybe I've eaten too much gravlax or taken too many trips to Ikea, but whenever I think of Scandinavian food, I think salmon and dill. This fried rice celebrates that dynamic duo, but I skip the usual addition of sour cream and use brown butter to add richness instead.

MAKES 4 SERVINGS

4 tablespoons unsalted butter, divided

1 pound salmon fillet, skin removed, cut into bite-size cubes

Kosher salt and freshly ground black pepper

8 ounces asparagus, ends trimmed, cut into 1-inch lengths

1 medium sweet onion, diced

2 cloves garlic, minced

4 cups cold cooked rice

Zest of 2 medium lemons

¼ cup freshly squeezed lemon juice (from 1 large lemon)

1 teaspoon kosher salt

¼ cup chopped fresh dill

1 lemon, cut into wedges

- Heat 3 tablespoons of butter in a large sauté pan over medium heat. Allow to cook until the milk solids turn golden brown and the butter smells nutty, about 2 minutes. Add the cubed salmon, sprinkle with salt and pepper, and sauté until lightly browned and cooked through, about 5 minutes. Transfer with a slotted spoon to a plate.

- Add the asparagus to the butter in the pan, sprinkle with salt and pepper, and sauté over medium-high heat, stirring only occasionally, until it begins to brown, about 5 minutes. Transfer to the plate with the salmon.

- Heat the remaining tablespoon of butter in the sauté pan over medium-high heat. Add the onion, sprinkle with salt and pepper, and sauté until tender, about 5 minutes. Add the garlic and sauté 1 minute more. Add the rice and sauté until warmed through and softened, then continue sautéing until the rice seems firm again, about 3 minutes. Stir in the lemon zest, lemon juice, and salt to taste. Add the salmon and asparagus to the pan and sauté until heated through.

- Divide among plates and garnish with fresh dill. Serve with lemon wedges.

Hungarian Goulash Fried Rice with Paprika, Caraway, and Cabbage

If you ask me, real Hungarian goulash puts traditional American beef stew to shame. It goes beyond being simply meaty by incorporating a heavy dose of paprika, tomatoes, and caraway seeds. It's a supremely comforting flavor combination, and when you use ground beef and tomato paste, it's easy to turn it into fried rice.

MAKES 4 SERVINGS

1 tablespoon caraway seeds

1 pound ground beef (80 percent lean)

1 teaspoon kosher salt, plus more to taste

¼ teaspoon freshly ground black pepper, plus more to taste

1 medium yellow onion, diced

1 large carrot, peeled and diced

1 green bell pepper, diced

3 large cloves garlic, minced

¼ cup tomato paste

2 tablespoons Hungarian paprika

2 tablespoons Worcestershire sauce

1 (15-ounce) can chopped tomatoes, drained (about 1 cup tomatoes)

2 teaspoons vegetable oil, plus more as needed

¼ head green cabbage, core removed, halved lengthwise, and thinly sliced crosswise (2 cups)

4 cups cold cooked Tomato Rice (page 44) or plain rice

Chopped fresh Italian parsley, for garnish

▪ Heat a large sauté pan over medium-high heat. Add the caraway seeds and toast until fragrant and slightly darkened, about 3 minutes. Remove from heat and transfer to a mortar and pestle or spice grinder, and grind them to a powder. Set aside.

▪ Return the pan to medium-high heat, and add the ground beef, salt, and pepper. Cook, stirring to break up the meat, until no longer pink, about 5 minutes. Use a slotted spoon to transfer the meat to a large bowl.

▪ Pour off all but 2 teaspoons of fat from the pan. Add the onion, carrot, and bell pepper. Season with salt and pepper. Sauté over medium-high heat until tender, about 7 minutes. Add the garlic and sauté about 1 minute more. Clear a space in the pan, and add the tomato paste. Cook the tomato paste until thicker and slightly darkened, about 3 minutes. Stir into the vegetables. Add the paprika,

Worcestershire sauce, and ground caraway and stir to combine. Add the tomatoes, then transfer the mixture to the bowl with the meat.

- Heat the oil in the same sauté pan over medium-high heat, add the cabbage, and season with salt and pepper. Sauté until wilted and beginning to brown, about 5 minutes. Add the rice and sauté until warmed through and softened, then continue sautéing until the rice seems firm again, about 3 minutes. Add the contents of the bowl and cook until evenly combined and warmed through. Taste and season with more salt and pepper if necessary.

- Divide rice among bowls, garnish with parsley, and serve.

Polish Fried Rice with Kielbasa and Cabbage

Kapusniak, a Polish soup of kielbasa, cabbage, and potatoes, goes on regular rotation at our house each winter. It's cheap, easy, hearty, and warming, and if you use good kielbasa (I use Portland-made Olympia Provisions), you can make it deeply flavorful with little effort. Turning it into a fried rice is as simple as skipping the broth and swapping rice for the potatoes. A handful of raw sauerkraut brightens it up and adds an extra hit of probiotic-rich nutrition.

MAKES 4 SERVINGS

2 teaspoons caraway seeds

1 (12-ounce) package kielbasa, diced

¼ head green cabbage, core removed, halved lengthwise, and thinly sliced crosswise (2 cups)

2 teaspoons olive or vegetable oil, plus more as needed

Kosher salt and freshly ground black pepper

1 medium yellow onion, diced

1 large carrot, peeled and diced

3 large cloves garlic, minced

1 tablespoon smoked paprika

4 cups cold cooked rice

¼ cup chopped fresh dill

1 cup raw sauerkraut, drained and chopped

1 cup sour cream, optional

▪ Heat a large sauté pan over medium-high heat. Add the caraway seeds and toast until fragrant and slightly darkened, about 3 minutes. Remove from heat and transfer to a mortar and pestle or spice grinder, and grind them to a powder. Set aside.

▪ Sauté the kielbasa in the same pan over medium-high heat until browned and fat has rendered, about 5 minutes; transfer to a medium bowl. Add the cabbage and a teaspoon of oil if needed, season with salt and pepper, and sauté until wilted and browned, about 5 minutes. Transfer to the bowl with the kielbasa.

▪ In the same pan, sauté the onion and carrot until tender, adding oil if needed, about 5 minutes. Add the garlic and sauté about 1 minute more. Season with salt and pepper, and add the paprika and ground caraway.

- Add a teaspoon of oil and the rice. Sauté over medium-high heat until warmed through and softened, then continue sautéing until the rice seems firm again, about 3 minutes. Add the ingredients from the bowl, stirring until evenly incorporated and warmed through. Remove from heat and fold in the dill. Taste and add more salt and pepper if necessary (keep in mind the sauerkraut will add salt).

- Divide fried rice among bowls. Top each with ¼ cup sauerkraut and sour cream.

Duck Confit Fried Rice with Fennel, Mustard Greens, and Pickled Currants

My favorite part of French cassoulet is the leg of duck confit. Few things are as incredibly rich and flavorful as duck meat cooked in its own delicious fat—especially when you add mustardy pickled currants and fragrant fennel. You can buy duck confit at upscale markets and online retailers, but it's not actually hard to make your own; it just takes time. You won't even need to source quarts of duck fat. Just follow the instructions on page 49.

MAKES 4 SERVINGS

PICKLED CURRANTS

1 teaspoon yellow mustard seeds
½ cup apple cider vinegar
½ cup water
3 sprigs fresh thyme
1 small shallot, thinly sliced
1 clove garlic, smashed
2 tablespoons packed dark brown sugar
1 teaspoon kosher salt
½ cup dried currants, raisins, or chopped prunes (see note)

FRIED RICE

2 confit duck legs (from Duck Leg Confit, page 49), or store-bought
4 ounces diced pancetta
1 medium yellow onion, diced
4 large cloves garlic, minced
1 tablespoon chopped fresh thyme
4 cups chopped mustard green leaves (about half a bunch, stemmed)
Kosher salt and freshly ground black pepper
4 cups cold cooked rice
1 tablespoon demi-glace (see note)
1 small fennel bulb, very thinly sliced with a mandoline (about 1 to 1½ cups)
¼ cup chopped fresh Italian parsley

▪ **TO MAKE THE PICKLED CURRANTS:** In a small saucepan, heat the mustard seeds over medium-high heat until they begin to pop, about 1 minute (you may want to use a splatter screen to keep them from launching out of the pan). Remove from heat and add the vinegar, water, thyme, shallot, garlic, sugar, and salt. Return to medium-high heat, bring to a simmer, and cook for about 5 minutes. Remove from heat and add the currants (if using prunes, wait until the mixture cools). Allow to cool, then transfer to an airtight container and allow the fruit to steep for at least 1 hour before using. (Can be made several weeks ahead and refrigerated.)

- **TO MAKE THE FRIED RICE:** Remove the skin from the duck legs and cut into ½-inch pieces. Pull the meat off the bones, shred, and set aside. You should have about 1½ cups.

- Heat a large sauté pan over medium-high heat, and set a paper-towel-lined plate nearby. Add the duck skin and cook until fat has rendered and skin is crispy, about 5 minutes. Use a slotted spoon to transfer the skin to the paper-towel-lined plate. Drain the duck fat from the pan and reserve.

- Return the sauté pan to medium-high heat. Add the pancetta and cook until crispy and fat has rendered, about 5 minutes. Transfer with a slotted spoon to the paper-towel-lined plate (but keep it separate from the duck skin).

- Pour off most of the fat in the pan, leaving about 2 teaspoons behind. Add the onion and sauté over medium-high heat until tender, about 5 minutes. Add the garlic and thyme and sauté about 1 minute more. Add the mustard greens and sauté until wilted, about 5 minutes. Season with salt and pepper to taste. Transfer the mixture to a medium bowl.

- Heat a teaspoon of reserved duck or pancetta fat in the same sauté pan. Add the rice and sauté until warmed through and softened, then continue sautóing until the rice seems firm again, about 3 minutes. Add the demi-glace and sauté until evenly incorporated. Add the shredded duck, pancetta, and the vegetables from the bowl, stirring until evenly distributed and warmed through.

- Divide fried rice among bowls. Top each with thinly sliced fennel, 2 tablespoons of pickled currants, crispy bits of duck skin, and a sprinkle of parsley.

NOTE: Feel free to use a combination of dried raisins, currants, and prunes. I actually prefer the flavor of pickled prunes in this dish, but regular supermarket prunes tend to be really moist, which makes for a rather mushy pickle. Try seeking out firm dried prunes (usually brands imported from Europe).

Demi-glace is super-concentrated stock. You can find little shelf-stable packages of the More Than Gourmet brand at well-stocked supermarkets. It's the secret ingredient to making this dish taste rich and almost luxurious, and it's a great way to beef up soups and pan sauces too.

Delicata and Kale Fried Rice with Rosemary, Agrodolce Raisins, and Parmesan

Delicata squash has so much going for it—namely, its pretty striped skin is thin enough that it doesn't need to be peeled. The sweet, firm flesh goes deliciously with Tuscan kale, rosemary, and a healthful blend of brown rice and cauliflower rice. To liven up these earthy flavors, I sprinkle this dish with golden raisins plumped in a sweet-sour mix of brown sugar and cider vinegar.

MAKES 4 SERVINGS

AGRODOLCE RAISINS

1 cup apple cider vinegar

½ cup packed dark brown sugar

1 sprig rosemary, chopped

½ teaspoon kosher salt

½ cup golden raisins

FRIED RICE

3 tablespoons extra-virgin olive oil, divided

1 large shallot, minced

4 large cloves garlic, minced

1 bunch Tuscan kale, stemmed, leaves thinly sliced (4 cups)

Kosher salt and freshly ground black pepper

1 small delicata squash, skin on, seeded and diced

3 to 4 tablespoons dry sherry or white wine

2 cups cauliflower rice

2 cups cold cooked brown rice

2 teaspoons minced fresh rosemary

1 cup finely grated Parmesan

¼ cup chopped toasted hazelnuts

▪ **TO MAKE THE RAISINS:** Heat the vinegar, brown sugar, rosemary, and salt in a small saucepan set over medium heat, stirring to dissolve the sugar. Bring to a simmer and cook for about 5 minutes. Remove from heat and add the raisins. Allow to cool, then transfer to an airtight container and allow the fruit to steep for at least 1 hour before using. (Can be made a week ahead and refrigerated.)

▪ **TO MAKE THE FRIED RICE:** Heat 1 tablespoon of the oil in a medium sauté pan over medium-high heat. Add the shallot and sauté until tender, about 3 minutes. Add the garlic and sauté 1 minute more. Add the kale and sauté until wilted, about 3 minutes. Season with salt and pepper. Transfer the mixture to a medium bowl.

$\longrightarrow$

- Heat another tablespoon of oil in the pan over medium-high heat. Add the squash, season with salt and pepper, and sauté until brown and tender, about 10 minutes, stirring occasionally. Deglaze the pan with the dry sherry, stirring to scrape up the browned bits. Transfer the squash to the bowl with the greens.

- Heat the remaining tablespoon of oil over medium-high heat. Add the cauliflower rice and brown rice. Sauté until heated through and beginning to take on a little color, about 5 minutes. Add the rosemary and season with salt. Add the greens and squash back to the pan; sauté until heated through.

- Divide the rice among plates and garnish with the Parmesan, hazelnuts, and drained pickled raisins to taste.

Carbonara Fried Rice

Rich, cheesy spaghetti carbonara studded with smoky bits of pork is my ultimate comfort food. Thankfully, it translates beautifully into fried rice. The biggest difference, aside from the lack of noodles, is that instead of whisking eggs into a sauce, I fry them up and use them to top the rice.

MAKES 4 SERVINGS

4 ounces diced pancetta, or 4 strips bacon, diced
1 medium yellow onion, diced
Kosher salt and freshly ground pepper
4 cloves garlic, minced
4 cups cold cooked rice
1 teaspoon freshly ground black pepper, plus more for garnish

1 ¼ ounce (½ cup packed) pecorino Romano cheese, finely grated on a Microplane, plus more for garnish
1 ounce (⅓ cup packed) Parmesan cheese, finely grated on a Microplane, plus more for garnish
4 eggs

■ Heat a large sauté pan over medium-high heat. Add the pancetta and cook until crisp and fat has rendered, about 5 minutes. Transfer the pancetta to a paper-towel-lined plate. Drain fat and reserve.

■ Heat 2 teaspoons of the pancetta fat in the same sauté pan. Add the onion, season with salt and pepper, and sauté until tender, about 5 minutes. Add the garlic and sauté about 1 minute more. Add the rice and sauté until warmed through and softened, then continue sautéing until the rice seems firm again, about 3 minutes. Add the pancetta and the teaspoon of pepper to the rice and season to taste with salt. Remove from heat and stir in the pecorino and Parmesan. Divide rice among bowls.

■ Wash and dry the sauté pan and return to medium-high heat (or use a different sauté pan). Add 2 more teaspoons of the pancetta fat. When hot, crack the eggs into the pan and fry for 2 minutes. Turn over and cook 1 minute more until whites are set and yolks are still runny. Top each serving of fried rice with a fried egg. Garnish with more cheese and pepper if desired.

Shrimp "Scampi" Fried Rice with Spinach

Technically, scampi is a variety of lobster-like crustacean, but the word has become synonymous with the Italian American dish of garlic, lemon, butter, and shrimp (hence the quote marks). I love making scampi with Oregon spot prawns when they're in season, but of course any good-quality shrimp would be delicious. Usually, this classic combination is tossed with linguini, but rice is even better at soaking up all the flavors.

MAKES 4 SERVINGS

3 tablespoons unsalted butter, divided
1 medium yellow onion, diced
8 cloves garlic, minced (about 2 tablespoons)
12 ounces peeled and deveined medium
   shrimp
Zest and juice of 1 medium lemon
Kosher salt and freshly ground black
   pepper

1 teaspoon Calabrian chili paste or red
   pepper flakes
1 (5-ounce) bag fresh baby spinach,
   chopped
4 cups cold Lemon Rice (page 42)
⅓ cup chopped fresh Italian parsley
Lemon wedges, for serving

▪ Heat 2 tablespoons of the butter in a large sauté pan over medium-high heat. Add the onion and sauté until tender, about 5 minutes. Add the garlic and sauté 1 minute more. Add the shrimp, lemon zest, and lemon juice. Season with salt and pepper and chilies or red pepper flakes. Sauté until shrimp are pink and opaque, about 3 minutes. Add the spinach and cook until wilted (add the spinach in batches if necessary so that it can fit in the pan), about 1 minute. Transfer the mixture to a medium bowl.

▪ Heat the remaining tablespoon of butter in the sauté pan, and add the rice. Sauté until warmed through and softened, then continue sautéing until the rice seems firm again, about 3 minutes. Add the ingredients from the bowl, leaving any accumulated liquid behind, which you can discard. Sauté until evenly incorporated and warmed through. Season with salt and pepper to taste.

▪ Divide fried rice among bowls. Garnish with parsley and lemon wedges.

Pancetta and Porcini Fried Risotto Balls (Arancini) with Fontina

For me, it isn't risotto without mushrooms, and one of the benefits of living in the Pacific Northwest is I can get fresh porcini mushrooms (called king boletes) on foraging hikes through the forest or at the farmers' market. I love their deep, savory flavor, and when they're not in season, I simply use dried. But there's one thing I don't do: stand around and stir. Risotto turns out just as rich and creamy when baked in the oven, which cuts your hands-on cooking time in half. This recipe makes a big batch of rich and savory mushroom risotto, so you can have some for dinner, then fry the rest into crispy arancini for your next party. No party in the near future? Just freeze the leftovers so they'll be ready whenever you are (give it a couple of days to defrost in the fridge). The arancini can even be formed several days in advance, then fried just in time to serve. The secret to the best arancini is adding some béchamel to the mix for creaminess and rolling them in a flour-based slurry, rather than egg, for a shatteringly crisp crust.

MAKES ABOUT 11 CUPS (enough for 4 servings of risotto, plus 16 risotto balls)

RISOTTO

8 cups low-sodium chicken broth

2 ounces dried porcini mushrooms (or 3 cups fresh; see note)

6 sprigs fresh thyme, tied with kitchen twine

2 bay leaves

8 ounces diced pancetta

2 large yellow onions, diced

4 teaspoons kosher salt, plus more for seasoning

Freshly ground black pepper

6 large cloves garlic, minced

1 pound (2½ cups) carnaroli or arborio rice

1 cup dry sherry or white wine

1 teaspoon freshly ground black pepper

4 tablespoons unsalted butter

2 ounces (1 cup) finely grated Parmesan, plus more for serving

½ cup chopped fresh Italian parsley

ARANCINI

1 tablespoon unsalted butter

2 tablespoons all-purpose flour

¾ cup whole milk

Kosher salt and freshly ground black pepper

2 cups leftover risotto

1 ounce (½ cup) finely grated Parmesan

½ cup all-purpose flour

½ cup water

4 cups panko

4 ounces fontina cheese, cut into ½-inch cubes

6 cups vegetable oil, for frying

Truffle salt

- **TO MAKE THE RISOTTO:** Bring the broth to a boil in a large saucepan, covered, over high heat. Turn off the heat and add the dried mushrooms. Cover and allow to rehydrate for 30 minutes. Strain through a fine-mesh sieve set over a large bowl, pressing on the mushrooms to extract the excess liquid. Set the bowl aside. Rinse the mushrooms under cold water to remove any remaining grit. Squeeze dry, then chop. Set aside.

- Rinse any grit from the saucepan and sieve. Carefully pour most of the broth through the sieve into the saucepan until you have about 1 cup left in the bowl. Line the sieve with a wet paper towel, and pour the remaining broth through it to catch the grit. Add the thyme bundle and bay leaves to the broth, cover the saucepan, and keep warm over low heat.

- Preheat oven to 350 degrees F. Heat a 6-quart Dutch oven over medium-high heat. Add the pancetta and cook until crispy and fat has rendered, 7 to 10 minutes. Transfer to a paper-towel-lined plate. Pour off all but 1 tablespoon of fat from the pot into a small bowl (it's flavorful, so save it in the fridge and use it to sauté something else).

- Return the pot to medium-high heat, and add the onions. Season with 1 teaspoon of salt and a few grinds of pepper. Sauté until onions are tender and have taken on some golden color, about 15 minutes (when they start sticking, reduce the heat to medium). Add the garlic and sauté about 1 minute more. Add the chopped rehydrated mushrooms, season with 1 teaspoon of salt and a few grinds of pepper, and sauté for 2 minutes.

- Add the rice to the pot and sauté until hot and beginning to look translucent around the edges, about 2 minutes. Add the sherry, little by little, to deglaze the pan, stirring to scrape up the browned bits. When the liquid is absorbed, pour in 7 cups of the hot broth, including the thyme sprigs and bay leaves. Season with 2 teaspoons of salt and 1 teaspoon of pepper. Cover, bring to a simmer, then transfer to the oven. Bake for 30 minutes, or until liquid is absorbed.

$\longrightarrow$

- Remove the thyme bundle and bay leaves. Stir in the butter, Parmesan, and pancetta. Remove two cups of risotto to use for arancini (allow to cool, then cover and refrigerate or freeze until ready to use. It will keep for several days refrigerated or several months frozen). Stir the remaining cup of broth into the rest of the risotto and season with salt and pepper to taste. Serve garnished with parsley, and pass more grated Parmesan at the table.

NOTE: If using fresh porcini mushrooms, dice the mushrooms, season with salt and pepper, and sauté in 1 tablespoon of pancetta fat until golden, about 7 minutes. Transfer to a plate and add to the risotto before baking.

- **TO MAKE THE ARANCINI:** Heat the butter in a large saucepan over medium-high heat until melted. Stir in the flour to make a roux. Cook, stirring, for about 1 minute, until bubbling. Slowly whisk in the milk, a little at a time, allowing the roux to absorb the liquid before adding more. Bring to a simmer and cook, stirring, for 2 minutes. Season with salt and pepper. Remove from heat and stir in the risotto. Allow to cool, stir in the Parmesan, then refrigerate for a couple of hours until completely cold. (Mixture can be made several days ahead and refrigerated.)

- In a medium bowl, whisk together the flour and water to make a thin paste. Pour the panko into a square baking dish or shallow bowl. Set a parchment-lined baking sheet nearby.

- Using a small, 2-inch-diameter ice cream scoop or a large spoon, portion out a meatball-size scoop of the chilled risotto mixture. Stuff a cube of fontina in the middle, sealing up the rice around it.

- Roll the ball into the flour paste until fully coated, then roll in the panko until fully coated. Make sure there aren't any bare spots or the risotto will leak through during frying. Set the arancini on the baking sheet, and repeat with the rest of the risotto. (Arancini can be prepared up to this point 3 days ahead; muffin tins work great as a holder for them. Cover and refrigerate until ready to fry.)

- Heat the oil in a deep, heavy-bottomed 6-quart saucepan or Dutch oven until it reaches 375 degrees F. Set a second baking sheet lined with paper towels or cooling racks nearby. Working in batches of about four at a time, carefully drop the arancini into the oil and fry until golden brown, about 3 minutes. Remove with a slotted spoon and transfer to the prepared baking sheet. Repeat with the remaining arancini. Sprinkle with truffle salt and serve while still warm.

Tuna Puttanesca Fried Rice

When I need a quick dinner, my thoughts immediately turn to pasta Puttanesca. It's built on staples I always have in my pantry—briny olives, capers, good albacore tuna, and anchovies—and they're bold enough that they need little else to quickly transform into a satisfying dish. When you have leftover rice on hand and not much in the fridge, this flavor-packed meal is your friend.

MAKES 4 SERVINGS

1 tablespoon extra-virgin olive oil, divided

1 medium red onion, diced

Kosher salt and freshly ground black pepper

4 large cloves garlic, minced

3 anchovies packed in oil

1 teaspoon crushed Calabrian chilies in oil or red pepper flakes

1 (15-ounce) can diced tomatoes, or 2 cups chopped fresh tomatoes

4 cups cold cooked rice, Lemon Rice (page 42), or Dashi Rice (page 39)

⅓ cup pitted kalamata or oil-cured olives, chopped

2 tablespoons capers, chopped

2 tablespoons chopped fresh basil, plus more for garnish

2 tablespoons chopped fresh Italian parsley, plus more for garnish

2 (5-ounce) cans solid albacore tuna, drained (see note)

- Heat 2 teaspoons of the oil in a large saucepan over medium high heat. Add the onion, season with salt and pepper, and sauté until tender, about 5 minutes. Add the garlic and sauté about 1 minute more. Clear a spot in the pan, and add the anchovies. Allow to cook while breaking them up with a wooden spoon until they become a liquidy paste, about 1 minute. Stir into the onions. Add the Calabrian chilies and tomatoes. Cook until the liquid is mostly evaporated, about 5 minutes.

- Heat the remaining teaspoon of oil in the pan. Add the rice and sauté until warmed through and softened, then continue sautéing until the rice seems firm again, about 3 minutes. Stir in the olives, capers, basil, and parsley. Flake the tuna and fold in. Cook until everything is heated through. Season with salt and pepper to taste.

- Divide among bowls and serve garnished with a sprinkle of herbs.

NOTE: Elemental dishes like this depend on high-quality ingredients. Get the best tuna you can. And if it's packed in oil, feel free to use some of the oil for sautéing the onions.

Paella Croquettes with Aioli

Seafood paella makes incredibly delicious croquettes, perfect for parties, but you can give any leftover rice dish the croquette treatment if you add a little egg and flour to bind the ingredients together. Like the arancini on page 128, this recipe is designed to provide dinner one night and leftovers you can fry into an appetizer or snack the next.

MAKES ABOUT 11 CUPS (ENOUGH FOR 4 SERVINGS OF PAELLA, PLUS 12 CROQUETTES)

AIOLI

1 clove garlic

1 egg

¾ cup extra-virgin olive oil

1 teaspoon kosher salt

2 tablespoons freshly squeezed lemon juice

PAELLA

7 cups fish broth or clam juice

Pinch of saffron, crushed (see note)

4 ounces Spanish chorizo, diced

1 large yellow onion, diced

1 red bell pepper, diced

1 green bell pepper, diced

2 Roma tomatoes, diced

3 cloves garlic, minced

½ pound squid, body and tentacles, cut into bite-size pieces

2 teaspoons smoked paprika

Kosher salt and freshly ground black pepper

½ cup dry sherry or white wine

3 cups bomba rice

½ pound peeled and deveined medium shrimp

½ cup piquillo peppers or roasted red peppers, cut into strips

⅓ cup chopped fresh Italian parsley

CROQUETTES

2 eggs

3 cups paella

2 tablespoons all-purpose flour

¼ cup vegetable oil

- **TO MAKE THE AIOLI:** In a food processor or blender, blend the garlic and egg until combined. Very slowly add the oil in a very thin, almost hair-like stream, until the mixture is emulsified. Pulse in the salt and 1 tablespoon of the lemon juice. Taste and add more lemon juice if desired. Transfer to an airtight container and refrigerate until ready to use. (Aioli will keep for several days in the refrigerator, so you'll be able to use it for both the paella dish and the croquettes.)

$\longrightarrow$

- **TO MAKE THE PAELLA:** Heat the fish broth in a medium saucepan, covered, set over medium-low heat. Stir the saffron into the hot broth. Keep warm.

- Heat a large sauté pan over medium-high heat. Add the chorizo and sauté until browned and oil has released, about 3 minutes. Add the onion, bell peppers, and tomatoes, and sauté until the vegetables are very soft and almost saucy, about 10 minutes, (reduce heat if necessary to keep from scorching). Add the garlic and sauté about 1 minute more. Add the squid and sauté until cooked through, about 2 minutes. Add the smoked paprika, and season with salt and pepper.

- Deglaze the pan with the sherry, stirring to scrape up the browned bits. Add the broth to the pan and bring to a boil over high heat. Add the rice, stir once to evenly distribute, and bring back to a boil. Reduce heat to medium-low and cook (do not stir) until liquid is mostly absorbed and rice is al dente, about 10 minutes. Nestle the shrimp into the rice, and arrange the pepper strips on top. Continue cooking until all the liquid has been absorbed and rice and shrimp are cooked through, about 10 more minutes.

- Remove from heat and cover with aluminum foil. Allow rice to steam for 10 minutes to help finish cooking the rice on top. Remove 3 cups of paella to use for croquettes (allow to cool, then cover and refrigerate or freeze until ready to use. It will keep for several days refrigerated or several months frozen). Serve the rest garnished with parsley and dollops of aioli.

- **TO MAKE THE CROQUETTES:** In a food processor, pulse the eggs until beaten. Add the paella and flour and pulse until combined (this helps chop up the paella ingredients).

- Heat the oil in a large sauté pan over medium heat. Working in batches of about 7 croquettes at a time, scoop ¼ cup of the paella mixture, form into a patty, then place in the hot pan. Allow to cook until golden brown, about 3 minutes. Turn over and cook until golden brown on the other side, about 3 minutes more. Transfer to a paper-towel-lined plate.

- Serve croquettes with aioli for dipping.

NOTE: If your saffron is too moist to crumble easily, lightly toast it in a dry pan over medium heat for about 1 minute (or microwave on a plate for about 1 minute). When it cools, it should be brittle enough to crumble. Crush it in a mortar and pestle or between two spoons.

ARROZ NEGRO VARIATION: To make squid ink paella (*arroz negro*) and croquettes, add 2 tablespoons of squid ink to the broth before adding the rice.

NOTE: Squid ink is usually found in small jars at gourmet markets or online retailers.

Grilled Greek Spanakorizo with Souvlaki Chicken

You don't have to fry rice on the stove. When it's hot out, take the skillet outside and cook it on the grill. This recipe turns *spanakorizo*, a traditional Greek dish of lemon-spinach rice, into fried rice, and pairs it with garlicky grilled skewers of *souvlaki*. You can skip the skewers and just grill whole chicken thighs on the grates, but the best part of souvlaki is the char, so don't be afraid to let them take on some color.

MAKES 4 SERVINGS

CHICKEN SOUVLAKI
Zest and juice of 1 medium lemon (¼ cup juice)

¼ cup extra-virgin olive oil

3 large cloves garlic, minced

1 tablespoon dried oregano

1 teaspoon kosher salt

½ teaspoon freshly ground black pepper

1 pound boneless, skinless chicken thighs, cut into 1-inch chunks

1 medium zucchini, cut into 1-inch chunks

1 medium red onion, cut into 1-inch chunks

FRIED RICE
1 tablespoon extra-virgin olive oil, divided

1 medium yellow onion, diced

4 large cloves garlic, minced

4 cups cold cooked Lemon Rice (page 42)

2 teaspoons ground cumin

4 ounces fresh baby spinach, chopped

Kosher salt and freshly ground black pepper

2 eggs, beaten

¼ cup chopped fresh dill

3 ounces (¾ cup) crumbled feta cheese

1 lemon, cut into wedges, for serving

■ **TO MAKE THE CHICKEN SOUVLAKI:** In a large bowl or ziplock bag, combine the lemon zest, lemon juice, olive oil, garlic, oregano, salt, and pepper. Add the chicken and zucchini and toss to coat. Allow to marinate at least 1 hour or up to overnight.

■ Prepare the grill for direct cooking over medium heat (350 to 450 degrees F). Brush the cooking grates clean. If you have a smoker box, add a handful of dry alder chips about 5 minutes before you start cooking.

$\longrightarrow$

Remove the chic
chicken, zucchini,
skewers soaked i
chicken is charre
platter, and cove

TO MAKE THE F
skillet set directl
the onion and s
1 minute more.
through and so
about 3 minute
spinach and co
Season with s

Push the ric
cleared area,
stirring, until
pan doesn't
the pan from

Divide the
skewers of

Classics of the Americas

/I\ \I/ /IN \I/ /IN \I/ /IN \I/ /IN \I/ /IN \I/ /IN \I/ /IN \I/

It's not that easy to define American cuisine. The dishes that typically represent "American food," from cheeseburgers to barbecue, are some kind of New World riff on a classic from somewhere else. But in a way, that's the beauty of it. What most iconic American dishes have in common isn't which ingredients or techniques they use, but rather a freedom to experiment. The recipes in this section take that theme and run with it, pulling from flavors south of the border too, and prove that just about anything can be turned into fried rice.

/IN \I/ /IN \I/ /IN \I/ /IN \I/ /IN \I/ /IN \I/ /IN \I/ /IN \I/

Huevos Rancheros Fried Rice

The rib-sticking breakfast of huevos rancheros was invented to use up leftover tortillas, so it's not such a stretch to apply the same logic to leftover rice. This version includes seared corn kernels and sautéed kale, so it's hearty enough to serve for dinner. The best part of huevos rancheros is the rich, spicy ranchero sauce, usually made by cooking grilled tomatoes, onions, and peppers into a sauce. To speed things up, I simply sauté store-bought *pico de gallo* with tomato paste and add canned chipotles in adobo sauce for smoke and spice.

MAKES 4 SERVINGS

2 tablespoons plus 1 teaspoon vegetable or
  extra-virgin olive oil, divided
1 medium yellow onion, diced
1 jalapeño or serrano pepper, minced
  (remove the seeds if you don't like heat)
4 cloves garlic, minced
½ bunch mustard greens or kale, stemmed,
  leaves chopped
Kosher salt and freshly ground black
  pepper

1 cup fresh or frozen corn kernels
¼ cup tomato paste
4 chipotles in adobo, chopped
1⅓ cup store-bought pico de gallo
4 cups cold cooked rice
4 eggs
½ cup chopped fresh cilantro
2 ounces (about ½ cup) crumbled cotija or
  feta cheese
1 avocado, sliced

▪ Heat 2 teaspoons oil in a large sauté pan over medium-high heat. Add the onion and jalapeño and sauté until tender, about 5 minutes. Add the garlic and sauté 1 minute more. Add the chopped greens, season with salt and pepper, and sauté until wilted and tender, about 5 minutes. Transfer to a medium bowl.

▪ Heat another teaspoon of oil in the sauté pan and add the corn. Sauté until browned, about 2 minutes; transfer to the bowl with the greens.

▪ Heat the tomato paste in the pan until slightly darkened and thicker, about 3 minutes. Add the chopped chipotles and pico de gallo. Cook, stirring, until the liquid has evaporated and the mixture is a thick, chunky sauce, about 2 minutes (if the pico de gallo is particularly dry, add a couple of tablespoons of water, or adobo sauce if you like more heat, to help create a saucy consistency). Transfer to a small bowl.

→

Buttermilk Buffalo Chicken Fried Rice

Even if you don't agree that ranch dressing and buffalo chicken are two of America's greatest contributions to gastronomy, you'll still love this crave-inducing fried rice. To capture that tangy-creamy buttermilk flavor I love about ranch without actually dousing my dinner in dressing, I cook the rice in buttermilk and use a packet of ranch dressing mix to season it up. I love this with spicy buffalo chicken, but if you don't love heat make the bacon-ranch variation instead.

MAKES 4 SERVINGS

BUFFALO CHICKEN

½ cup buttermilk

½ cup Frank's RedHot sauce (try not to substitute another brand; this one has the perfect balance of heat and vinegary tang)

1 tablespoon plus 1 teaspoon ranch dressing powder, divided

2 boneless, skinless chicken breasts, or 4 boneless, skinless chicken thighs, cut into ¾-inch cubes

1 cup rice flour

1 tablespoon vegetable or extra-virgin olive oil, plus more as needed

FRIED RICE

2 teaspoons extra-virgin olive oil or vegetable oil

1 medium yellow onion, diced

3 cloves garlic, minced

4 cups cold Buttermilk Rice (page 42) or plain rice

1 teaspoon ranch dressing powder

1⅓ cups frozen peas and carrots

2 green onions, ends trimmed, chopped

▪ **TO MAKE THE BUFFALO CHICKEN:** In a medium bowl, combine the buttermilk, hot sauce, and 2 teaspoons of the ranch powder. Transfer ⅓ cup of the marinade to a small bowl, cover, and refrigerate until ready to use when making the fried rice. Add the chicken to the rest of the marinade in the bowl, toss to coat evenly, cover, and refrigerate for at least 2 hours (up to overnight).

▪ In a wide shallow bowl, combine the rice flour and remaining 2 teaspoons of ranch powder. Use a slotted spoon to remove the chicken from the marinade, shaking off the excess. Drop the chicken in the rice flour, a few pieces at a time, and toss to coat. Set the floured pieces of chicken on a wire cooling rack to dry out for at least 20 minutes (this will help the coating adhere to the chicken and fry up crisp).

$\longrightarrow$

- Heat the oil in a large sauté pan (preferably nonstick) over medium-high heat. Add the chicken in an even layer without crowding and sear until browned on one side, about 3 minutes. Turn the pieces over and brown on the other side, about 3 minutes more. (If your pan isn't big enough to arrange the chicken without crowding, brown it in batches, adding more oil as necessary. Otherwise it will steam instead of brown.) Transfer chicken to a plate as you go.

- **TO MAKE THE FRIED RICE:** Heat the oil in the same sauté pan over medium-high heat (if the pan was very sticky after cooking the chicken, wash and dry it first). Add the onion and sauté until tender, about 5 minutes. Add the garlic and sauté about 1 minute more. Add the rice and ranch powder, then sauté until rice is heated through and starting to firm up a bit, about 3 minutes. Add the peas and carrots and sauté until heated through. Add ¼ cup of the reserved marinade and sauté until rice is evenly coated. Taste and add more marinade if desired. Stir in the chicken and sauté until warmed through.

- Divide fried rice among plates and serve garnished with chopped green onions. Pass more Frank's hot sauce at the table.

BUTTERMILK BACON-RANCH VARIATION: Omit the hot sauce from the marinade. Dice 4 slices of bacon and sauté in a large pan over medium-high heat until crisp. Transfer to a paper-towel-lined plate, and pour off all but 1 tablespoon of bacon grease from the pan. Sauté floured chicken in the bacon grease. Proceed with the rest of the recipe, adding the bacon to the fried rice when you add the cooked chicken. Serve the rice with 2 tablespoons of chopped fresh dill and a drizzle of ranch dressing or squeeze of lemon.

Cajun BBQ Shrimp Fried Rice

In New Orleans, BBQ shrimp has nothing to do with actual barbecues. In fact, the shrimp never even get close to a grill. Instead, "BBQ" refers to the buttery Cajun-spiced sauce the shrimp are sautéed in. It's so good, you'll want to lick the pan. Luckily, the rice soaks up every last drop.

MAKES 4 SERVINGS

- 3 tablespoons unsalted butter, divided
- 1 medium yellow onion, diced
- 3 cloves garlic, minced
- 2 teaspoons Worcestershire sauce
- 1½ teaspoons Creole seasoning (such as Cajun's Classic Seasoning)
- 1 teaspoon Hungarian paprika
- 8 ounces peeled and deveined medium shrimp
- 2 tablespoons freshly squeezed lemon juice
- 1 tablespoon Crystal Hot Sauce, plus more for serving
- 4 green onions, ends trimmed, white and light-green parts cut into 1-inch lengths
- 8 ounces (about 2 cups) green beans, cut into 1-inch pieces
- 4 cups cold cooked rice
- Kosher salt and freshly ground black pepper

- Heat 2 tablespoons of the butter in a large sauté pan over medium-high heat. Add the onion and sauté until tender, about 5 minutes. Add the garlic and sauté about 1 minute more. Add the Worcestershire sauce, Creole seasoning, and paprika, stirring to combine. Add the shrimp, lemon juice, and hot sauce. Cook until shrimp are pink and opaque, about 3 minutes. Transfer mixture to a bowl.

- Heat the remaining tablespoon of butter in the sauté pan. Add the green onions and green beans; sauté until browned, about 5 minutes. Add the rice and sauté until warmed through and softened, then continue sautéing until the rice seems firm again, about 3 minutes. Add the ingredients from the plate, stirring until evenly incorporated and warmed through. Season with salt and pepper to taste.

- Divide rice among plates. Pass more Crystal Hot Sauce at the table.

Cheeseburger Fried Rice

When I told my husband I wanted to turn cheeseburgers into fried rice, he just screwed up his face and shook his head. He's a burger addict and could not imagine his favorite food translating into fried rice form. I'll admit that this isn't the same as sinking your teeth into a juicy burger, but with its mustardy tomato rice and pickly fry sauce, this dish tastes just like the real thing. In fact, it's my husband's hands-down favorite recipe in this book. So when you're craving a burger but don't have (or want) a bun, this recipe has you covered.

MAKES 4 SERVINGS

FRY SAUCE

⅓ cup mayonnaise

3 tablespoons ketchup

2 tablespoons dill pickle relish or finely
  diced dill pickles

2 teaspoons apple cider vinegar

FRIED RICE

1 pound ground beef (90 percent lean)

2 tablespoons Worcestershire sauce

2 teaspoons kosher salt

½ teaspoon garlic powder

1 teaspoon vegetable oil

1 large yellow onion, diced

2 large cloves garlic, minced

4 cups cold Tomato Rice (page 44; see
  note)

3 tablespoons yellow mustard

4 slices American cheese

1 heart of romaine lettuce, cut crosswise
  into ribbons

1 cup cherry tomatoes, quartered

▪ **TO MAKE THE FRY SAUCE:** Mix the mayonnaise, ketchup, relish, and vinegar together in a small bowl. (If not using right away, cover and refrigerate; fry sauce will keep for about 1 week.)

▪ **TO MAKE THE FRIED RICE:** Heat a large sauté pan over medium-high heat. Add the beef and cook, breaking it up, until no longer pink, about 5 minutes. Add the Worcestershire sauce, salt, and garlic powder and cook 1 minute more. Transfer to a plate. (If the meat was fatty, transfer meat with a slotted spoon and drain the fat from the pan.)

$\longrightarrow$

- Heat the oil in the same pan, and add the onion. Sauté until tender, about 5 minutes. Add the garlic and sauté about 1 minute more. Add the rice and 2 tablespoons of the fry sauce to the pan, and sauté until rice is heated through and starting to firm up a bit, about 3 minutes. Add the mustard and cook, stirring until well combined. Add the meat to the rice and cook until heated through.

- Divide rice among plates and top with a slice of American cheese, a small handful of lettuce, cherry tomatoes, and fry sauce.

NOTE: If you have a hankering for this dish but don't have Tomato Rice on hand, you can use cold cooked white rice and add ¼ cup tomato paste when sautéing the rice with the onions.

Taco Salad Fried Rice

I grew up eating gringo tacos—the ones with the hard corn shell filled with ground beef mysteriously seasoned with a packet. They're not the least bit like true Mexican street tacos, but they have their place in the world and in my heart. This recipe ditches the corn shell for fried rice, but it has the same addictive combination of seasoned beef, crispy lettuce, juicy tomato, and black olives. If you don't have all these spices in your pantry, a packet of taco seasoning will suffice.

MAKES 4 SERVINGS

1 pound lean ground beef (90 percent lean)
2 tablespoons plus 1 teaspoon chili powder
3 teaspoons ground cumin
1 to 2 teaspoons kosher salt
2 teaspoons ground chipotle powder
2 teaspoons Mexican oregano
1 teaspoon ground coriander
1 teaspoon onion powder
1 teaspoon garlic powder
1 medium yellow onion, diced
Kosher salt and freshly ground pepper
3 cloves garlic, minced

4 cups cold cooked rice
1 cup frozen corn
1 heart of romaine lettuce, cut crosswise into ribbons
½ cup store-bought pico de gallo
1 avocado, diced
2 tablespoons canned sliced black olives, roughly chopped
2 tablespoons pickled jalapeños, roughly chopped
½ cup sour cream

- Heat a large sauté pan over medium-high heat. Add the beef and cook, breaking it up, until no longer pink, about 5 minutes. Add the chili powder, cumin, salt, chipotle powder, oregano, coriander, onion powder, and garlic powder and cook 1 minute more. Transfer to a plate and drain off all but 2 teaspoons of fat from the pan (or add 2 teaspoons of vegetable oil if there's no leftover fat).

- Add the onion to the sauté pan, season with salt and pepper, and sauté over medium-high heat until tender, about 5 minutes. Add the garlic and sauté about 1 minute more. Add the rice to the pan and sauté until warmed through and softened, then continue sautéing until the rice seems firm again, about 3 minutes. Add the frozen corn and cook until heated through, about 2 minutes. Add the meat back to the pan and sauté until heated through.

- Divide rice among plates and top with lettuce, pico de gallo, avocado, olives, jalapeños, and a dollop of sour cream.

Ham and Cheese Fried Rice with Basil Pesto

Generally speaking, if a combination of ingredients works as a sandwich, it'll work as fried rice. Even ham and cheese. The trick is to shop wisely. This is no place for wet, soggy deli meat. Go for real artisan ham that you can buy in a thick slab and dice. For the cheese, nothing beats halloumi, a semisoft Cyprian cheese, for sheer crispy-gooey cookability. It somehow manages to hold its shape even when sautéed or grilled.

MAKES 4 SERVINGS

1 ounce (about ½ cup) grated sharp cheddar cheese
2 ounces halloumi cheese, cut into ½-inch-thick slices
⅓ pound good-quality ham, cut into ½-inch cubes
Vegetable or extra-virgin olive oil, as needed for sautéing
1 medium yellow onion, diced
2 cloves garlic, minced

4 cups cold cooked rice
2 to 3 tablespoons store-bought or homemade basil pesto
2 teaspoons Dijon mustard
1 cup frozen peas and carrots
Kosher salt and freshly ground black pepper
1 cup cherry tomatoes, halved or quartered
1 green onion, ends trimmed, thinly sliced

- Set a large nonstick sauté pan over medium-high heat. Set a paper-towel-lined plate nearby. When the pan is hot, add about 1 tablespoon of shredded cheese, spreading it out a bit to make a small circle. Allow to cook for 1 to 2 minutes, until the cheese is melted and the edges are golden. Use a thin spatula to turn the frico over, and cook the other side until firm, about 30 seconds more. Transfer to the paper-towel-lined plate and set aside. Repeat with the rest of the cheese.

- Pat the halloumi dry, and add it to the same pan. Sear over medium-high heat until brown on one side, 1 to 2 minutes. Carefully turn the slices over and brown the other side, 1 to 2 minutes more. Transfer to a cutting board. Allow to cool for about a minute, then cut into bite-size cubes.

- Add the ham to the same sauté pan (there should be oil in the pan that was released from the cheeses; if not, add a teaspoon of vegetable oil) and sauté until browned, 3 to 4 minutes. Remove with a slotted spoon, leaving the fat behind, and transfer to a plate.

- Add the onion to the same pan and sauté until tender, about 5 minutes. Add the garlic and sauté about 1 minute more. If the pan seems dry, add a teaspoon of oil. Add the rice and sauté until warmed through and softened, then continue sautéing until the rice seems firm again, about 3 minutes. Stir in 2 tablespoons of the pesto and the mustard until evenly incorporated. Taste and add another tablespoon of pesto if desired.

- Add the peas and carrots, ham, and halloumi to the pan and cook until heated through. Season with salt and pepper to taste.

- Divide rice among plates and top with cherry tomatoes, crumbled cheddar frico, and a sprinkle of green onions.

Hawaiian Spam and Pineapple Fried Rice

Spam *musubi*, that genius Hawaiian creation of barely sweet sushi rice topped with a slab of salty Spam and wrapped in a belt of briny seaweed, should be in the snacking Hall of Fame. It hits all my most dire cravings all in one go. This fried rice aims to re-create that simple pleasure, with a drizzle of homemade teriyaki sauce and little fresh pineapple thrown in for bright pops of sweetness.

MAKES 4 SERVINGS

2 tablespoons extra-virgin olive oil, divided

4 cloves garlic, minced, divided

1 (2-inch) piece fresh ginger, peeled and grated (1 tablespoon)

½ cup low-sodium Aloha shoyu or soy sauce (see note)

¼ cup packed dark brown sugar

2 tablespoons mirin

1 tablespoon rice vinegar

10 ounces Spam (preferably low-sodium), diced

8 green onions, ends trimmed, white and light-green parts cut into 1-inch lengths

1 medium yellow onion, diced

4 cups cold cooked rice

1 cup frozen peas and carrots (optional)

1 cup finely diced fresh pineapple

4 small sheets of roasted seaweed, cut crosswise with scissors into thin strips

▪ Heat 1 teaspoon of the olive oil in a small saucepan over medium heat. Add half the garlic and sauté about 1 minute. Add the ginger, shoyu, brown sugar, and mirin. Bring to a boil, reduce to a simmer, and cook until thickened and reduced to ⅓ cup, about 7 minutes. Remove from heat, add the rice vinegar, and allow to cool.

▪ Heat 2 teaspoons of oil in a large sauté pan over medium-high heat. Add the diced Spam and sauté until browned and seared, about 5 minutes. Transfer to a medium bowl. Add the green onions to the same pan and sauté until just beginning to brown, about 2 minutes. Transfer to the bowl with the Spam.

$\longrightarrow$

- Heat another 2 teaspoons of oil in the same sauté pan over medium-high heat. Add the onion, season with salt and pepper, and sauté until tender, about 5 minutes. Add the remaining garlic and sauté about 1 minute more. Add the remaining teaspoon of oil and the rice. Sauté until warmed through and softened, then continue sautéing until the rice seems firm again, about 3 minutes. Add the sautéed spam and green onions from the bowl, and the peas and carrots. Stir in about ¼ cup of the reserved sauce and sauté until evenly coated. Remove from heat, and stir in the pineapple.

- Divide mixture among plates and top with seaweed. Pass the remaining sauce at the table.

NOTE: Aloha shoyu and Aloha soy sauce are sweeter and milder than regular soy sauce, and staples of Hawaiian dishes. They're easy to find, but if you don't want to buy something just for this, low-sodium soy sauce works great too.

Garlicky Bacon, Egg, and Avocado Fried Rice

This easy fried rice is a great utility player, able to go from breakfast to lunch to dinner without a hitch. Flavor-wise, it's a lot like home fries, even though there's not a single potato in sight. I like to sear the avocado, which adds a crispy layer of light char to the creamy flesh. And the sweet-sour heat of Mama Lil's peppers really completes the dish. You can order this Northwest native online if you can't find it in stores near you. Or substitute spicy marinated cherry peppers.

MAKES 4 SERVINGS

4 strips bacon, diced
1 large avocado, cut into ½-inch cubes
1 medium yellow onion, diced
4 cloves garlic, minced
4 cups cold cooked rice
½ teaspoon chili powder
½ teaspoon smoked paprika
½ teaspoon kosher salt

¼ teaspoon garlic powder
¼ teaspoon onion powder
4 eggs
⅓ cup diced Mama Lil's Sweet Hot Peppas or hot cherry peppers in oil
⅓ cup chopped fresh chives or green onion tops

▪ Heat a large sauté pan over medium-high heat. Add the bacon and cook until crisp and fat has rendered, about 5 minutes. Transfer to a paper-towel-lined plate. Drain fat and reserve.

▪ Heat 1 teaspoon of the bacon fat in the same pan over medium-high heat. Add the avocado and cook, turning occasionally, until brown on all sides, about 1 minute per side. Transfer to a plate.

$\longrightarrow$

▪ Heat another teaspoon of the bacon fat in the same pan. Add the onion and sauté until tender, about 6 minutes. Add the garlic and sauté 1 minute more. Add the rice and sauté until warmed through and softened, then continue sautéing until the rice seems firm again, about 3 minutes. Stir in the chili powder, smoked paprika, salt, garlic powder, and onion powder. Add the bacon and avocado to the rice, gently tossing to evenly distribute. Divide mixture among plates.

▪ Wash and dry the pan and return to medium-high heat (or use a different sauté pan). Add 2 teaspoons of bacon fat. When hot, crack the eggs into the pan and fry for 2 minutes. Turn over and cook 1 minute more until whites are set and yolks are still runny. Top each serving of fried rice with a fried egg. Garnish with diced peppers and chives.

Rainbow Veggie Fried Rice with Tofu

If you want to pack your plate with a rainbow of veggies, this vegan fried rice is for you. Follow the recipe as written, or feel free to use whatever vegetables you have on hand. I like to pan-sear the tougher vegetables to bring out their inner sweetness, while simply sautéing the more tender stuff. Don't skip out on pressing the tofu. It allows the tofu to soak up more flavor and gives it a firmer, meatier texture. The flavor-packed sauce incorporates the greatest hits of my favorite Asian condiments and works with just about any stir-fry you can imagine.

MAKES 4 SERVINGS

1 (14-ounce) package firm tofu

¼ cup plus 2 tablespoons Bragg Liquid Aminos, divided

2 tablespoons *gochujang*

1 tablespoon sambal oelek

1 tablespoon mirin

1 tablespoon Chinese black vinegar (Chinkiang)

1 tablespoon rice vinegar

1 to 2 teaspoons packed dark brown sugar (optional)

2 tablespoons plus 1 teaspoon vegetable oil

1 cup broccoli florets

⅛ head green cabbage, core removed, halved lengthwise, and thinly sliced crosswise (1 cup)

4 ounces (about ½ cup) green beans, cut into 1-inch lengths

½ yellow bell pepper, diced

½ red bell pepper, diced

1 medium yellow onion, diced

¾ cup peeled, diced carrot (about 1 large)

3 large cloves garlic, minced

4 cups cold cooked brown rice

Kosher salt and freshly ground black pepper

▪ Cut the tofu lengthwise into ¾-inch-thick slabs. Arrange on a clean dish towel and set another dish towel on top. Set a baking sheet weighted with cans on top of the tofu. Allow to sit for 10 minutes to press out the excess liquid. Cut the pressed tofu into ¾-inch cubes and transfer to a large bowl. Sprinkle with ¼ cup of the Bragg's, tossing to evenly distribute.

▪ In a small bowl, mix together the remaining 2 tablespoons of Bragg's, gochujang, sambal oelek, mirin, black vinegar, rice vinegar, and sugar if using. Set aside.

⟶

- Heat a large sauté pan over medium-high heat. Add 1 teaspoon of the oil and the broccoli. Sauté until tender-crisp and browned in places, 5 to 7 minutes. Transfer to another large bowl. Add another teaspoon of oil to the pan and the cabbage. Sauté until browned in places and wilted, about 5 minutes. Transfer to the bowl with the broccoli. Add another teaspoon of oil to the pan and the green beans and bell peppers. Sauté until tender-crisp, about 3 minutes. Transfer to the bowl of vegetables.

- Heat 1 tablespoon of the oil in the pan and add the tofu, tossing to coat the cubes in the oil. Allow to sear until golden, about 1 minute, then use tongs to turn and sear the other sides until golden, about 1 minute per side. Transfer to the bowl of vegetables.

- Add the remaining teaspoon of oil to the pan, and add the onion and carrot. Sauté until tender, about 5 minutes. Add the garlic and sauté 1 minute more. Add the rice and sauté until warmed through and softened, then continue sautéing until the rice seems firm again, about 3 minutes. Add the vegetables and tofu from the bowl and sauté until warmed through. Drizzle with the sauce, stirring until evenly incorporated. Taste and season with salt and pepper.

- Divide rice among bowls and serve.

A Sweet Finish

When it comes to transforming leftover rice into something sweet, rice pudding always comes to mind—and with good reason. It's creamy, sweet, and comforting. But pudding is just the beginning. With a little ingenuity, rice can form the basis for an array of creative desserts (just look at *mochi*, for example). It's naturally sweet after all. This section stays true to the "fried leftover rice" theme with five really different ways to give your rice a sweet send-off.

Puffed-Rice PB & J Bars

Homemade puffed rice is so much more ricey flavored than crisped rice cereal, and these fast and easy peanut-buttery treats are a great way to show it off. Instead of the usual corn syrup, I use Lyle's Golden Syrup, which has a far richer, almost toffee-like flavor. It's easy to get online, at World Market, or at well-stocked grocery stores. To add fruity-jammy notes while preserving the crunch factor, I fold in crispy freeze-dried berries. Look for them in the snack aisle; even Target has them.

MAKES ABOUT 16 (2-INCH) SQUARES

Unsalted butter, for greasing dish
½ cup packed dark brown sugar
½ cup Lyle's Golden Syrup
½ cup smooth peanut butter
2 teaspoons pure vanilla extract
1 teaspoon kosher salt, plus more to taste

4 cups Puffed Rice (page 47)
1 ounce (1½ cups) freeze-dried strawberries or raspberries (or other freeze-dried fruit, such as bananas), divided
Sea salt, for garnish

▪ Butter an 8-inch square baking dish. Heat the sugar and syrup in a medium saucepan set over medium heat, stirring until mixture is melted and sugar is dissolved, about 2 minutes. Remove from heat and stir in the peanut butter, vanilla, and salt until smooth and combined. Stir in the puffed rice and half the freeze-dried fruit.

▪ Press into the prepared baking dish in an even layer, then press the remaining fruit on top. Sprinkle with sea salt. Allow to sit until firm, about 1 hour, before cutting into 2-inch squares. Squares will keep in an airtight container for several days.

Brown-Butter Apple and Cinnamon Fried Rice with Candied Nuts

Let's say you have a little leftover rice on hand and you've got a craving for something sweet. Just sauté it up with cinnamon, maple syrup, and apples. But if you really want to turn it into dessert, serve it with a scoop of ice cream. Seriously, rice and ice cream go surprisingly well together, and a handful of chopped candied nuts adds all-important crunch.

MAKES 4 SERVINGS

CANDIED NUTS

1 tablespoon unsalted butter

1 cup roughly chopped raw walnuts, pecans, or hazelnuts

¼ cup packed dark brown sugar

Kosher salt

FRIED RICE

1 tablespoon unsalted butter

1 firm apple (such as Fuji, Honeycrisp, or Granny Smith) or Asian pear, peeled, cored, and cut into ¼-inch dice (about 1 cup)

⅛ teaspoon ground cinnamon

Pinch of ground nutmeg

½ cup cold cooked rice

1 teaspoon maple syrup

Vanilla ice cream (optional)

▪ **TO MAKE THE NUTS:** Set a piece of parchment or a Silpat near the stove. Melt the butter in a medium sauté pan set over medium heat. Add the nuts and sauté until beginning to brown and smell toasty, about 3 minutes. Add the brown sugar and sauté until the sugar melts and coats the nuts, and you just start to smell burnt sugar, no more than 1 minute. Immediately remove from heat and scrape the nuts onto the parchment paper. Sprinkle lightly with salt. Allow to cool until crisp.

▪ **TO MAKE THE FRIED RICE:** Return the sauté pan to the stove. Melt the butter over medium-high heat and allow to cook, stirring occasionally, until the milk solids turn brown and the butter smells nutty, about 1 minute.

▪ Immediately add the apple pieces and sauté, stirring once or twice, until they are seared and golden, about 5 minutes. Sprinkle with cinnamon and nutmeg. Add the rice and sauté until warmed through, about 3 minutes. Add the maple syrup and sauté until evenly absorbed.

▪ Divide the rice among bowls and top with the candied nuts and a scoop of ice cream.

Horchata Crepes with Bananas and Rum

Though they're only technically fried, these sweet cinnam___
way to use up leftover rice. Your house will smell like *hor*___
the addition of rice gives them a little bit more heft than r___
eat them plain, just swiped with butter and sprinkled with___
sugar, or go over the top with sautéed bananas and whip___

MAKES ABOUT 10 CREPES

CREPES
½ cup cold cooked rice
1½ cups whole milk
3 eggs
1¼ cups all-purpose flour
1 tablespoon granulated sugar
½ teaspoon ground cinnamon
1 teaspoon vanilla
¼ teaspoon kosher salt
1 to 2 tablespoons melted unsalted butter

BANANA-R___
2 tablespoon___
2 tablespoon___
   divided
4 bananas, p___
2 tablespoon___
Pinch of kosl___
1 cup heavy___

- **TO MAKE THE CREPES:** Place rice and milk in a blend___
process until smooth, about 1 minute. Add the eggs, fl___
vanilla, and salt. Process until smooth. Let the batter re___
(or refrigerate for up to 2 days) before using.

- Preheat an 8-inch nonstick skillet over medium-high___
minutes. Brush the pan lightly with melted butter. Pou___
the hot pan, wait a few seconds, then tilt the pan in al___
batter into an even circle.

$\longrightarrow$

New Orleans Calas with Spiced Sugar

Light-as-air beignets get all the attention in the Big Easy, but these yeast-risen fritters have a much better story. Historians say some slaves were able to buy their freedom by selling *calas*. It was also a means for former slaves to make a living. Clearly, that's some very significant dough, in both senses of the word. I'm all for keeping this flame of history alive by frying calas up on the regular, and the fact that they taste like the best doughnut holes you've ever had is just icing on the cake. I use a little less egg than traditional recipes to keep them super light. And I roll them in spiced sugar instead of powered because, well, that's how I roll.

MAKES ABOUT 2 DOZEN

SPICED SUGAR
½ cup granulated sugar
2 teaspoons ground cinnamon
⅛ teaspoon ground cardamom
⅛ teaspoon ground allspice
Pinch of kosher salt

CALAS
1 (¼-ounce) packet active dry yeast
1 cup warm water (120 degrees F)
2 eggs
½ cup packed dark brown sugar
2 tablespoons dark rum
1 teaspoon nutmeg
½ teaspoon kosher salt
2 cups cold cooked rice
2 cups all-purpose flour
6 cups vegetable oil, for frying

- **TO MAKE THE SPICED SUGAR:** Combine the sugar, cinnamon, cardamom, allspice, and salt in a medium bowl. Set aside.

- **TO MAKE THE CALAS:** In a small glass measuring cup, combine the yeast and warm water. Allow to sit until yeast is dissolved, about 5 minutes.

- In medium mixing bowl, whisk the eggs, brown sugar, rum, nutmeg, and salt until well combined. Stir in the rice and yeast mixture. Fold in the flour. Cover with a clean dish cloth and allow to sit at room temperature overnight (about 8 hours). If you are not using the batter right away, cover with plastic wrap and refrigerate until ready to use.

$\longrightarrow$

- Heat the vegetable oil in a large saucepan set over medium-high [it] it reaches 350 degrees F. Set cooling racks or a baking sheet lined towels nearby. And have the spiced sugar ready. Working in batche[s] five at a time, drop the batter by the tablespoon into the hot oil. Fry, needed, until evenly golden, about 2 minutes. Remove with a slotte[d] transfer to the cooling racks. Roll in the spiced sugar while still warr[m] with the remaining batter. Calas are best eaten while still warm.

- Cook over medium heat until the top is dry and edges are starting to brown, about 1 minute. Loosen the edges with the tip of a spatula, slide it underneath the crepe, and carefully turn the crepe over. Cook the other side until browned, about 30 seconds. Slide the crepe onto a plate and repeat with the remaining batter, stacking the cooked crepes. (Crepes can be made several days ahead, covered, and refrigerated. Reheat in a sauté pan over medium heat until warm, about 1 minute.)

- **TO MAKE THE BANANA FILLING:** Melt 1 tablespoon of the butter and 1 tablespoon of the sugar in a large sauté pan over medium-high heat. Add half the bananas in an even layer and sauté until beginning to brown, 1 to 2 minutes. Turn over and sauté the other side until beginning to brown, about 1 minute more. Add 1 tablespoon of the rum and sauté for about 1 minute to cook off some of the alcohol (or, if you're adventurous, light it with a match and let the flames die down on their own). Season with a pinch of salt. Transfer to a medium bowl and repeat with the remaining butter, sugar, bananas, rum, and salt.

- Spoon a little banana filling into each of the warm crepes, fold in half or quarters, and spoon a little more on top. Add a dollop of whipped cream and serve.

Deep-Fried Rice Pudding

Savory arancini are such a great way to use up leftover risotto and turn it into an appetizer or snack. Why not use the same logic and turn leftover plain rice into a sweet treat? I love using leftover rice to make rice pudding, but here I've taken it a step further by turning it into a handheld dessert that's great for parties. If you have time, soak the raisins in rum or bourbon before using.

MAKES ABOUT 2 DOZEN 2-INCH BALLS

2½ cups cold cooked plain rice or Coconut
   Rice (page 43)
2 tablespoons cornstarch
½ cup packed dark brown sugar
2 eggs
2 cups whole milk
½ cup raisins (optional; see note)
¾ teaspoon ground cinnamon, divided

¼ teaspoon ground nutmeg
Pinch of kosher salt
1 teaspoon vanilla extract
½ cup all-purpose flour
½ cup plus 2 tablespoons water
2 cups panko
4 to 6 cups vegetable oil, for frying
¼ cup granulated sugar

- In a medium saucepan, combine the rice and cornstarch until rice is evenly dusted (this helps prevent lumps). Mix in the brown sugar, eggs, milk, raisins, ¼ teaspoon of the cinnamon, nutmeg, and salt. Set the pan over medium heat and cook, stirring frequently, until mixture thickens, 10 to 12 minutes. Remove from heat, stir in the vanilla, and transfer to a medium bowl. Allow to cool, then refrigerate until cold, about 3 hours. (Mixture can be made several days ahead and refrigerated.)

- In another medium bowl, whisk together the flour and water to make a slurry. Pour the panko into a wide, shallow dish. Set a large cooling rack or parchment-lined baking sheet nearby.

- Using a tablespoon, portion out a scoop of the rice pudding mixture. Shape into a ball, then roll it in the slurry until fully coated, lifting it out with a fork and tapping on the side of the bowl to let the excess drip off. Set the ball in the dish of panko and roll to coat. Make sure there aren't any bare spots or the rice will leak through during frying. Set the ball on the cooling rack or baking sheet and repeat with the rest of the pudding. (Pudding balls can be prepared up to this point 3 days ahead; muffin tins work great as a holder for them. Cover and refrigerate until ready to fry.)

- Heat the oil in a deep, 6-quart, heavy-bottomed saucepan or Dutch oven until it reaches 350 degrees F. Set another baking sheet lined with paper towels or cooling racks nearby. Working in batches of about four at a time, carefully drop the balls into the oil and fry until golden brown, about 2 minutes. Remove with a slotted spoon and transfer to the baking sheet or cooling rack. Repeat with the remaining balls.

- In a small bowl, combine the granulated sugar and remaining ½ teaspoon of cinnamon. Roll the balls in the spiced sugar while still warm and serve.

NOTE: I love raisins in rice pudding, but you can leave them out if that's not your thing. Another option: allow the raisins to soak for an hour in heated dark rum, spiced rum, or bourbon to cover. Strain and stir into the pudding before you refrigerate it. Save the liquor for another use, such as cocktails, baked goods, or a boozy milkshake.

Acknowledgments

The cool thing about writing a single-subject cookbook is you get to dive deep into a narrow niche and see how far you can go. But it also requires dogged determination and vast amounts of patience from friends and family who, unlike you, didn't sign up to eat the same ingredient seven days a week for months.

And so, I offer my unending gratitude to my husband, Mike, who never complained that there were rice grains in every crevice of the kitchen, and always offered honest feedback even if it meant yet another round of fried rice. And to my daughters Emma and Audrey, who learned to stop asking, "What's for dinner?" and only rolled their eyes a handful of times. I feel incredibly lucky to have such a supportive family and constructively critical audience.

I also offer big thanks to publisher Gary Luke for entrusting me with the project, and to the rest of the team at Sasquatch Books for bringing it all to life.

I'm deeply grateful to my friend and fellow cookbook author Jen Stevenson, who generously opened the door to this project and also took time out to test a recipe. And, of course, the rest of my crack team of recipe testers proved invaluable once again: Abbie Rankin, Brad Hart, Christina Perron, Christopher Mullins, Cory Raiton, Hannah Wallace, JoAnna Rodriguez, Juno DeMelo, Keith Sheets, Sandi Francioch, Sasha Kaplan, Shannon Pickens, and Stephanie Booth. Their excellent taste and exacting judgment ensured these recipes will turn out deliciously, and I couldn't have done this book without them.

Index

Page numbers in italics indicate photos

A

the Americas, 141
  Bacon, Corn, and Crab
    Fried Rice with Sweet
    Peppers, 168–69
  BBQ Fried Rice with Soy
    Curls and Spicy Slaw,
    152–53
  Buttermilk Buffalo Chicken
    Fried Rice, *148,* 149–50
  Cajun BBQ Shrimp Fried
    Rice, 151
  Cheeseburger Fried Rice,
    154, 155–56
  Chorizo and Egg Fried
    Rice with Radishes and
    Avocado, 145
  Garlicky Bacon, Egg, and
    Avocado Fried Rice,
    163–64
  Ham and Cheese Fried Rice
    with Basil Pesto, 158–59
  Hawaiian Spam and
    Pineapple Fried Rice, *160,*
    161–62
  Huevos Rancheros Fried
    Rice, *142,* 143–44
  New Mexican Chili Fried
    Rice with Queso and
    Pork, 146–47
  Rainbow Veggie Fried Rice
    with Tofu, 165–66, *167*
  Taco Salad Fried Rice, 157
**Arancini (Pancetta and Porcini
  Fried Risotto Balls) with
  Fontina,** 128–30

**Arroz Negro (variation of
  Paella Croquettes with
  Aioli),** 135
Asian inspiration, 55–85
  Burmese Fried Rice with
    Chicken, Herbs, and
    Crispy Shallots, 78, *79*
  Classic Chinese Fried Rice
    with BBQ Pork, *56,* 57
  Filipino Fried Rice
    (Sinangag) with Adobo
    Chicken, 84–85
  Japanese Chahan with
    Shrimp, Dashi Rice, and
    Kombu Tsukudani, 60–61
  Korean Kimchi and Bulgogi
    Fried Rice, 82–83, *83*
  Nam Khao Tod with Pork
    Larb, 72–73
  Nasi Goreng (Indonesian
    Fried Rice), 80–81
  Pad Thai Fried Rice with
    Shrimp and Spinach,
    69–70, *71*
  Smoky Lapsang Souchong
    Fried Rice with Duck
    Breast and Hoisin Sauce,
    62–63
  Spicy Fried Rice with
    Chinese Broccoli, Ground
    Pork, and Szechuan Chili
    Oil, 58–59
  Thai Fried Coconut Rice
    with Pork Satay and
    Spinach, *74,* 75–76, *77*

  Vietnamese Pho Fried Rice
    with Beef, Cilantro, and
    Bean Sprouts, 64–65
  Vietnamese Pork Meatball
    Banh Mi Fried Rice, *66,*
    67–68
asparagus
  Salmon and Asparagus
    Fried Rice with Lemon
    and Fresh Dill, *114,* 115
avocado(s)
  Chorizo and Egg Fried
    Rice with Radishes and
    Avocado, 145
  Garlicky Bacon, Egg, and
    Avocado Fried Rice,
    163–64
  Huevos Rancheros Fried
    Rice, *142,* 143–44
  Taco Salad Fried Rice, 157

B

bacon. *See also* pancetta
  Bacon, Corn, and Crab
    Fried Rice with Sweet
    Peppers, 168–69
  Garlicky Bacon, Egg, and
    Avocado Fried Rice,
    163–64
**BBQ Fried Rice with Soy Curls
  and Spicy Slaw,** 152–53
beans and legumes
  Jollof Fried Rice with
    Chakalaka, 93–94
  Mujadara Fried Rice,
    95–96, *97*

bean sprouts
  Pad Thai Fried Rice with
    Shrimp and Spinach,
    69–70, 71
  Vietnamese Pho Fried Rice
    with Beef, Cilantro, and
    Bean Sprouts, 64–65
beef
  Cheeseburger Fried Rice,
    154, 155–56
  Hungarian Goulash Fried
    Rice with Paprika,
    Caraway, and Cabbage,
    116–17
  Jollof Fried Rice with
    Chakalaka, 93–94
  Korean Kimchi and Bulgogi
    Fried Rice, 82–83, 83
  Lubia Polow (Persian Green
    Bean Rice with Beef),
    106–09, 107
  Taco Salad Fried Rice, 157
  Vietnamese Pho Fried Rice
    with Beef, Cilantro, and
    Bean Sprouts, 64–65
bonito flakes, 28
  Crispy Soy-Glazed Bonito
    Flakes (Okaka), 48
Bragg Liquid Aminos, 28
broccoli. See also Chinese
  broccoli
  Rainbow Veggie Fried Rice
    with Tofu, 165–66, 167
Brown-Butter Apple and
  Cinnamon Fried Rice with
  Candied Nuts, 174
brown rice, 15
  Steamed Brown Rice, 38
Burmese Fried Rice with
  Chicken, Herbs, and Crispy
  Shallots, 78, 79

Buttermilk Rice, 42–43
  Buttermilk Bacon-Ranch
    Chicken Fried Rice
    (variation of Buttermilk
    Buffalo Chicken Fried
    Rice), 150
  Buttermilk Buffalo Chicken
    Fried Rice, 148, 149–50

C

cabbage. See also napa
  cabbage
  BBQ Fried Rice with Soy
    Curls and Spicy Slaw,
    152–53
  Hungarian Goulash Fried
    Rice with Paprika,
    Caraway, and Cabbage,
    116–17
  Jollof Fried Rice with
    Chakalaka, 93–94
  Polish Fried Rice with
    Kielbasa and Cabbage,
    118–19, 119
  Rainbow Veggie Fried Rice
    with Tofu, 165–66, 167
Cajun BBQ Shrimp Fried Rice,
  151
Calabrian chilies, 28
Carbonara Fried Rice, 125
cashews
  Chitranna (Indian Lemon
    Rice) with Curry Leaves
    and Cashews, 91–92
cauliflower rice, 33
  Delicata and Kale Fried
    Rice with Rosemary,
    Agrodolce Raisins, and
    Parmesan, 122, 123–24
  Fried Cauliflower Rice with
    Turkey Kofta, Mint, and
    Feta, 98, 99

Fried Rice with Halloumi,
  Pickled Onions, and
  Zhug, 102, 103–05
cheese
  Carbonara Fried Rice, 125
  Cheeseburger Fried Rice,
    154, 155–56
  Delicata and Kale Fried
    Rice with Rosemary,
    Agrodolce Raisins, and
    Parmesan, 122, 123–24
  Fried Cauliflower Rice with
    Turkey Kofta, Mint, and
    Feta, 98, 99
  Fried Rice with Halloumi,
    Pickled Onions, and
    Zhug, 102, 103–05
  Ham and Cheese Fried Rice
    with Basil Pesto, 158–59
  New Mexican Chili Fried
    Rice with Queso and
    Pork, 146–47
  Pancetta and Porcini Fried
    Risotto Balls (Arancini)
    with Fontina, 128–30
Cheeseburger Fried Rice, 154,
  155–56
chicken
  Burmese Fried Rice with
    Chicken, Herbs, and
    Crispy Shallots, 78, 79
  Buttermilk Buffalo Chicken
    Fried Rice, 148, 149–50
  Chitranna (Indian Lemon
    Rice) with Curry Leaves
    and Cashews, 91–92
  Filipino Fried Rice
    (Sinangag) with Adobo
    Chicken, 84–85
  Grilled Greek Spanakorizo
    with Souvlaki Chicken,
    136, 137–38, 139

Moroccan Fried Rice with
Chicken, Saffron, and
Figs, 100–01
Nasi Goreng (Indonesian
Fried Rice), 80–81
Vagharelo Bhaat (Gujarati
Fried Rice) with Chicken
and Cilantro Yogurt, *88,*
89–90
Chinese broccoli. *See also*
broccoli
Spicy Fried Rice with
Chinese Broccoli, Ground
Pork, and Szechuan Chili
Oil, 58–59
**Chinese Fried Rice with BBQ
Pork**, Classic, *56, 57*
**Chinkiang vinegar (Chinese
black vinegar)**, 28–29
chipotles in adobo, 29
**Chitranna (Indian Lemon
Rice)** with Curry Leaves and
Cashews, 91–92
chorizo, 29
Chorizo and Egg Fried
Rice with Radishes and
Avocado, 145
Coconut Rice, 43
Thai Fried Coconut Rice
with Pork Satay and
Spinach, *74,* 75–76, *77*
converted/parboiled rice, 14
cooking methods
Instant Pot (electric
pressure cooker), 21–23
microwave, 21
oven, 23
rice cooker, 20
stir-frying, 23–24
stovetop, 21
cooking tools, 24–28, *26–27*

corn
Bacon, Corn, and Crab
Fried Rice with Sweet
Peppers, 168–69
BBQ Fried Rice with Soy
Curls and Spicy Slaw,
152–53
Huevos Rancheros Fried
Rice, *142,* 143–44
New Mexican Chili Fried
Rice with Queso and
Pork, 146–47
Taco Salad Fried Rice, 157
crab
Bacon, Corn, and Crab
Fried Rice with Sweet
Peppers, 168–69
**Crispy Soy-Glazed Bonito
Flakes (Okaka)**, 48
curry leaves
Chitranna (Indian Lemon
Rice) with Curry Leaves
and Cashews, 91–92

D
dashi
Kombu Dashi Rice, 39–40
deep-fried treats
Deep-Fried Rice Pudding,
180–81
Nam Khao Tod with Pork
Larb, 72–73
New Orleans Calas with
Spiced Sugar, 175–76,
176
Pancetta and Porcini Fried
Risotto Balls (Arancini)
with Fontina, 128–30
**Delicata and Kale Fried Rice
with Rosemary, Agrodolce
Raisins, and Parmesan**, *122,*
123–24

desserts. *See* sweets and
desserts
Diamond Crystal Kosher Salt,
29–30
duck
Duck Confit Fried Rice with
Fennel, Mustard Greens,
and Pickled Currants,
120–21
Duck Leg Confit, 49–50
Smoky Lapsang Souchong
Fried Rice with Duck
Breast and Hoisin Sauce,
62–63

E
eggs
Carbonara Fried Rice, 125
Chorizo and Egg Fried
Rice with Radishes and
Avocado, 145
Garlicky Bacon, Egg, and
Avocado Fried Rice,
163–64
Huevos Rancheros Fried
Rice, *142,* 143–44
**Europe and the
Mediterranean**, 111–39
Carbonara Fried Rice, 125
Delicata and Kale Fried
Rice with Rosemary,
Agrodolce Raisins, and
Parmesan, *122,* 123–24
Duck Confit Fried Rice with
Fennel, Mustard Greens,
and Pickled Currants,
120–21
Grilled Greek Spanakorizo
with Souvlaki Chicken,
136, 137–38, *139*

Hungarian Goulash Fried
Rice with Paprika,
Caraway, and Cabbage,
116–17
Leek and Wild Mushroom
Fried Rice, 112, *113*
Paella Croquettes with Aioli,
132, 133–35, *135*
Pancetta and Porcini Fried
Risotto Balls (Arancini)
with Fontina, 128–30
Polish Fried Rice with
Kielbasa and Cabbage,
118–19, *119*
Salmon and Asparagus
Fried Rice with Lemon
and Fresh Dill, *114,* 115
Shrimp "Scampi" Fried Rice
with Spinach, 126, *127*
Tuna Puttanesca Fried Rice,
131

F
fennel
Duck Confit Fried Rice with
Fennel, Mustard Greens,
and Pickled Currants,
120–21
figs
Moroccan Fried Rice with
Chicken, Saffron, and
Figs, 100–01
Filipino Fried Rice (Sinangag)
with Adobo Chicken, 84–85
fish and seafood
Bacon, Corn, and Crab
Fried Rice with Sweet
Peppers, 168–69
Cajun BBQ Shrimp Fried
Rice, 151

Japanese Chahan with
Shrimp, Dashi Rice, and
Kombu Tsukudani, 60–61
Nasi Goreng (Indonesian
Fried Rice), 80–81
Pad Thai Fried Rice with
Shrimp and Spinach,
69–70, *71*
Paella Croquettes with Aioli,
132, 133–35, *135*
Salmon and Asparagus
Fried Rice with Lemon
and Fresh Dill, *114,* 115
Shrimp "Scampi" Fried Rice
with Spinach, 126, *127*
Tuna Puttanesca Fried Rice,
131
fish sauce, 30
**Fried Cauliflower Rice with
Turkey Kofta, Mint, and
Feta,** *98,* 99
fried onions or shallots, 30
fried rice
advantages of, 9–10
origins of, 9
using day-old rice, 16
**Fried Rice with Halloumi,
Pickled Onions, and Zhug,**
102, 103–05
frozen peas and carrots
Buttermilk Buffalo Chicken
Fried Rice, *148,* 149–50
Ham and Cheese Fried Rice
with Basil Pesto, 158–59
Hawaiian Spam and
Pineapple Fried Rice, *160,*
161–62
fruit
Brown-Butter Apple and
Cinnamon Fried Rice with
Candied Nuts, 174

Horchata Crepes with
Bananas and Rum,
177–78, *179*
Puffed-Rice PB & J Bars,
172, *173*

G
**Garlicky Bacon, Egg, and
Avocado Fried Rice,** 163–64
glutinous rice, 14
gochugaru, 30
gochujang, 30
green beans
Cajun BBQ Shrimp Fried
Rice, 151
Lubia Polow (Persian Green
Bean Rice with Beef),
106–09, *107*
greens
BBQ Fried Rice with Soy
Curls and Spicy Slaw,
152–53
Delicata and Kale Fried
Rice with Rosemary,
Agrodolce Raisins, and
Parmesan, *122,* 123–24
Duck Confit Fried Rice with
Fennel, Mustard Greens,
and Pickled Currants,
120–21
Huevos Rancheros Fried
Rice, *142,* 143–44
**Grilled Greek Spanakorizo
with Souvlaki Chicken,** *136,*
137–38, *139*
**Gujarati Fried Rice (Vagharelo
Bhaat) with Chicken and
Cilantro Yogurt,** *88,* 89–90

H

halloumi, 30

ham

Ham and Cheese Fried Rice
with Basil Pesto, 158–59

Hawaiian Spam and
Pineapple Fried Rice, *160,*
161–62

herbs

Burmese Fried Rice with
Chicken, Herbs, and
Crispy Shallots, 78, *79*

Delicata and Kale Fried
Rice with Rosemary,
Agrodolce Raisins, and
Parmesan, *122,* 123–24

Duck Confit Fried Rice with
Fennel, Mustard Greens,
and Pickled Currants,
120–21

Fried Cauliflower Rice with
Turkey Kofta, Mint, and
Feta, *98,* 99

Fried Rice with Halloumi,
Pickled Onions, and
Zhug, *102,* 103–05

Nam Khao Tod with Pork
Larb, 72–73

Salmon and Asparagus
Fried Rice with Lemon
and Fresh Dill, *114,* 115

Vietnamese Pho Fried Rice
with Beef, Cilantro, and
Bean Sprouts, 64–65

Vietnamese Pork Meatball
Banh Mi Fried Rice, *66,*
67–68

hoisin sauce, 30–31

Horchata Crepes with
Bananas and Rum, 177–78,
179

Huevos Rancheros Fried Rice,
142, 143–44

Hungarian Goulash Fried Rice
with Paprika, Caraway, and
Cabbage, 116–17

I

India, Africa, and the Middle
East, 87–109

Chitranna (Indian Lemon
Rice) with Curry Leaves
and Cashews, 91–92

Fried Cauliflower Rice with
Turkey Kofta, Mint, and
Feta, *98,* 99

Fried Rice with Halloumi,
Pickled Onions, and
Zhug, *102,* 103–05

Jollof Fried Rice with
Chakalaka, 93–94

Lubia Polow (Persian Green
Bean Rice with Beef),
106–09, *107*

Moroccan Fried Rice with
Chicken, Saffron, and
Figs, 100–01

Mujadara Fried Rice,
95–96, *97*

Vagharelo Bhaat (Gujarati
Fried Rice) with Chicken
and Cilantro Yogurt, *88,*
89–90

Indian chili powder, 31

**Indian Lemon Rice (Chitranna)
with Curry Leaves and
Cashews**, 91–92

**Indonesian Fried Rice (Nasi
Goreng)**, 80–81

J

Japanese Chahan with
Shrimp, Dashi Rice, and
Kombu Tsukudani, 60–61

Japanese Soy-Preserved
Kombu (Kombu Tsukudani),
49

Jollof Fried Rice with
Chakalaka, 93–94

K

kecap manis, 31

kimchi, 31

Korean Kimchi and Bulgogi
Fried Rice, 82–83, *83*

kombu, 31

Japanese Chahan with
Shrimp, Dashi Rice, and
Kombu Tsukudani, 60–61

Japanese Soy-Preserved
Kombu (Kombu
Tsukudani), 49

Kombu Dashi Rice, 39–40

**Korean Kimchi and Bulgogi
Fried Rice**, 82–83, *83*

**Koshari (variation of Mujadara
Fried Rice)**, 96, *97*

L

Lapsang Souchong Rice, 40,
41

Lapsang Souchong Fried
Rice with Duck Breast
and Hoisin Sauce, Smoky,
62–63

leek(s)

Leek and Wild Mushroom
Fried Rice, 112, *113*

lemon(s)

Chitranna (Indian Lemon
Rice) with Curry Leaves
and Cashews, 91–92

Grilled Greek Spanakorizo
with Souvlaki Chicken,
136, 137–38, 139
Lemon Rice, 42
Preserved Lemons, 51
Salmon and Asparagus
Fried Rice with Lemon
and Fresh Dill, *114,* 115
Shrimp "Scampi" Fried Rice
with Spinach, 126, *127*
lentils
Mujadara Fried Rice,
95–96, *97*
lettuce
Cheeseburger Fried Rice,
154, 155–56
Taco Salad Fried Rice, 157
long-grain rice, 11–12
basmati, 11–12
jasmine, 12
Lubia Polow (Persian Green
Bean Rice with Beef),
106–09, *107*

M
medium-grain rice, 12
Bhutanese red, 12
Calrose, 12
forbidden (black), 12
sushi, 12
Middle Eastern Spice Mix, 52
mirin, 31
Moroccan Fried Rice with
Chicken, Saffron, and Figs,
100–01
Mujadara Fried Rice, 95–96,
97
mushroom(s)
Leek and Wild Mushroom
Fried Rice, 112, *113*

Pancetta and Porcini Fried
Risotto Balls (Arancini)
with Fontina, 128–30

N
Nam Khao Tod with Pork Larb,
72–73
nam prik pao, 31–32
napa cabbage. *See also*
cabbage
Burmese Fried Rice with
Chicken, Herbs, and
Crispy Shallots, 78, *79*
Nasi Goreng (Indonesian Fried
Rice), 80–81
New Mexican Chili Fried
Rice with Queso and Pork,
146–47
New Orleans Calas with
Spiced Sugar, 175–76, *176*
nuts
Brown-Butter Apple and
Cinnamon Fried Rice with
Candied Nuts, 174
Chitranna (Indian Lemon
Rice) with Curry Leaves
and Cashews, 91–92

O
Okaka (Crispy Soy-Glazed
Bonito Flakes), 48

P
Pad Thai Fried Rice with
Shrimp and Spinach, 69–70,
71
Paella Croquettes with Aioli,
132, 133–35, *135*
palm sugar, 32
pancetta, 32. *See also* bacon
Carbonara Fried Rice, 125

Pancetta and Porcini Fried
Risotto Balls (Arancini)
with Fontina, 128–30
panko, 32
pantry items, 28–36
parboiled/converted rice, 14
peppers
Bacon, Corn, and Crab
Fried Rice with Sweet
Peppers, 168–69
Jollof Fried Rice with
Chakalaka, 93–94
New Mexican Chili Fried
Rice with Queso and
Pork, 146–47
Paella Croquettes with Aioli,
132, 133–35, *135*
Rainbow Veggie Fried Rice
with Tofu, 165–66, *167*
Persian Green Bean Rice with
Beef (Lubia Polow), 106–09,
107
pineapple
Hawaiian Spam and
Pineapple Fried Rice, *160,*
161–62
plum sauce, 32
Polish Fried Rice with Kielbasa
and Cabbage, 118–19, *119*
pork
Classic Chinese Fried Rice
with BBQ Pork, *56,* 57
Hawaiian Spam and
Pineapple Fried Rice, *160,*
161–62
Nam Khao Tod with Pork
Larb, 72–73
New Mexican Chili Fried
Rice with Queso and
Pork, 146–47

Spicy Fried Rice with
Chinese Broccoli, Ground
Pork, and Szechuan Chili
Oil, 58–59
Thai Fried Coconut Rice
with Pork Satay and
Spinach, *74, 75–76, 77*
Vietnamese Pho Fried Rice
with Beef, Cilantro, and
Bean Sprouts, 64–65
Vietnamese Pork Meatball
Banh Mi Fried Rice, *66,
67–68*
Preserved Lemons, 51
Puffed Rice, *46, 47*
Puffed-Rice PB & J Bars,
172, *173*

R
radishes
Chorizo and Egg Fried
Rice with Radishes and
Avocado, 145
**Rainbow Veggie Fried Rice
with Tofu**, 165–66, *167*
raisins and currants
Delicata and Kale Fried
Rice with Rosemary,
Agrodolce Raisins, and
Parmesan, *122,* 123–24
Duck Confit Fried Rice with
Fennel, Mustard Greens,
and Pickled Currants,
120–21
rice, 33. *See also* specific
types of rice
buying and storing, 15–16
cooking liquid, 17–18
freezing cooked, 23
as a pantry item, 33
rinsing, 18–20

salting, 20
steaming after cooking, 20
yield, 18
riced vegetables, 33
Rice Pudding, Deep-Fried,
180–81

S
salmon
Salmon and Asparagus
Fried Rice with Lemon
and Fresh Dill, *114,* 115
sambal oelek, 33
sausage
Chorizo and Egg Fried
Rice with Radishes and
Avocado, 145
Paella Croquettes with Aioli,
132, 133–35, *135*
Polish Fried Rice with
Kielbasa and Cabbage,
118–19, *119*
shallots
Burmese Fried Rice with
Chicken, Herbs, and
Crispy Shallots, 78, *79*
Shatta Sauce, 52
short-grain rice, 12–14
arborio, 12–14
bomba, 14
carnaroli, 12–14
vialone nano, 12–14
shrimp
Cajun BBQ Shrimp Fried
Rice, 151
Japanese Chahan with
Shrimp, Dashi Rice, and
Kombu Tsukudani, 60–61
Nasi Goreng (Indonesian
Fried Rice), 80–81

Pad Thai Fried Rice with
Shrimp and Spinach,
69–70, *71*
Shrimp "Scampi" Fried Rice
with Spinach, 126, *127*
shrimp paste, 33
**Shrimp "Scampi" Fried Rice
with Spinach**, 126, *127*
**Sinangag (Filipino Fried Rice)
with Adobo Chicken**, 84–85
**Smoky Lapsang Souchong
Fried Rice with Duck Breast
and Hoisin Sauce**, 62–63
**Soy-Glazed Bonito Flakes
(Okaka), Crispy**, 48
**Spicy Fried Rice with Chinese
Broccoli, Ground Pork, and
Szechuan Chili Oil**, 58–59
spinach
Chitranna (Indian Lemon
Rice) with Curry Leaves
and Cashews, 91–92
Grilled Greek Spanakorizo
with Souvlaki Chicken,
136, 137–38, *139*
Mujadara Fried Rice,
95–96, *97*
Pad Thai Fried Rice with
Shrimp and Spinach,
69–70, *71*
Shrimp "Scampi" Fried Rice
with Spinach, 126, *127*
Thai Fried Coconut Rice
with Pork Satay and
Spinach, *74, 75–76, 77*
squash
Delicata and Kale Fried
Rice with Rosemary,
Agrodolce Raisins, and
Parmesan, *122,* 123–24

squid
    Paella Croquettes with Aioli,
       132, 133–35, *135*
Steamed Brown Rice, 38
Steamed White Rice, 37–38
sweets and desserts, 171–81
    Brown-Butter Apple and
       Cinnamon Fried Rice with
       Candied Nuts, 174
    Deep-Fried Rice Pudding,
       180–81
    Horchata Crepes with
       Bananas and Rum,
       177–78, *179*
    New Orleans Calas with
       Spiced Sugar, 175–76,
       176
    Puffed-Rice PB & J Bars,
       172, *173*
Szechuan chili flakes/chili
    powder, 33
    Spicy Fried Rice with
       Chinese Broccoli, Ground
       Pork, and Szechuan Chili
       Oil, 58–59
Szechuan peppercorns, 36

T
Taco Salad Fried Rice, 157
tamarind concentrate, 36
tea
    Lapsang Souchong Rice,
       40, *41*
Thai Fried Coconut Rice with
    Pork Satay and Spinach, *74,*
    75–76, *77*
Thai red curry paste, 36
tofu
    Rainbow Veggie Fried Rice
       with Tofu, 165–66, *167*

tomato(es)
    Cheeseburger Fried Rice,
       154, 155–56
    Hungarian Goulash Fried
       Rice with Paprika,
       Caraway, and Cabbage,
       116–17
    Jollof Fried Rice with
       Chakalaka, 93–94
    Tomato Rice, 44, *45*
    Tuna Puttanesca Fried Rice,
       131
truffle salt, 36
Tuna Puttanesca Fried Rice,
    131
turkey
    Fried Cauliflower Rice with
       Turkey Kofta, Mint, and
       Feta, *98,* 99

V
Vagharelo Bhaat (Gujarati
    Fried Rice) with Chicken
    and Cilantro Yogurt, *88,*
    89–90
vegan meat alternatives
    BBQ Fried Rice with Soy
       Curls and Spicy Slaw,
       152–53
    Chorizo and Egg Fried
       Rice with Radishes and
       Avocado, 145
    Rainbow Veggie Fried Rice
       with Tofu, 165–66, *167*
Vietnamese Pho Fried Rice
    with Beef, Cilantro, and
    Bean Sprouts, 64–65
Vietnamese Pork Meatball
    Banh Mi Fried Rice, *66,*
    67–68

W
White Rice, Steamed, 37–38
wild rice, 15

Y
yuzu essence, 36

Printed in China

SASQUATCH BOOKS with colophon is a registered trademark of Penguin Random House LLC

23 22 21 20 19   9 8 7 6 5 4 3 2 1

Editor: Gary Luke
Production editor: Jill Saginario
Design: Tony Ong
Photographs: Audrey Kelly
Food Styling: Isabel Thottam
Copyeditor: Erin Cusick

Library of Congress Cataloging-in-Publication Data
Names: Centoni, Danielle, author.
Title: Fried rice : 50 ways to stir up the world's favorite grain / Danielle Centoni.
Description: Seattle, WA : Sasquatch Books, 2019 | Includes index.
Identifiers: LCCN 2018059070 | ISBN 9781632172297 (hard cover)
Subjects: LCSH: Fried rice. | Cooking (Rice) | LCGFT: Cookbooks.
Classification: LCC TX809.R5 C43 2019 | DDC 641.6/318--dc23
LC record available at https://lccn.loc.gov/2018059070

ISBN: 978-1-63217-229-7

Sasquatch Books
1904 Third Avenue, Suite 710
Seattle, WA 98101

SasquatchBooks.com

Conversions

VOLUME			LENGTH		WEIGHT	
UNITED STATES	METRIC	IMPERIAL	UNITED STATES	METRIC	AVOIRDUPOIS	METRIC
¼ tsp.	1.25 mL		⅛ in.	3 mm	¼ oz.	7 g
½ tsp.	2.5 mL		¼ in.	6 mm	½ oz.	15 g
1 tsp.	5 mL		½ in.	1.25 cm	1 oz.	30 g
½ Tbsp.	7.5 mL		1 in.	2.5 cm	2 oz.	60 g
1 Tbsp.	15 mL		1 ft.	30 cm	3 oz.	90 g
⅛ c.	30 mL	1 fl. oz.			4 oz.	115 g
¼ c.	60 mL	2 fl. oz.			5 oz.	150 g
⅓ c.	80 mL	2.5 fl. oz.			6 oz.	175 g
½ c.	125 mL	4 fl. oz.			7 oz.	200 g
1 c.	250 mL	8 fl. oz.			8 oz. (½ lb.)	225 g
2 c. (1 pt.)	500 mL	16 fl. oz.			9 oz.	250 g
1 qt.	1 L	32 fl. oz.			10 oz.	300 g

TEMPERATURE				11 oz.	325 g
OVEN MARK	FAHRENHEIT	CELSIUS	GAS	12 oz.	350 g
Very cool	250–275	130–140	½–1	13 oz.	375 g
Cool	300	150	2	14 oz.	400 g
Warm	325	165	3	15 oz.	425 g
Moderate	350	175	4	16 oz. (1 lb.)	450 g
Moderately hot	375	190	5	1½ lb.	750 g
	400	200	6	2 lb.	900 g
Hot	425	220	7	2¼ lb.	1 kg
	450	230	8	3 lb.	1.4 kg
Very hot	475	245	9	4 lb.	1.8 kg